SBN 361 03874 7
Maps © 1977 Vallardi Industrie Grafiche.
Published 1977 by Purnell Books, Berkshire House,
Queen Street, Maidenhead, Berkshire.
Text © 1977 Purnell and Sons Limited
Reprinted 1979, 1980

Purnell's Illustrated
Nature Atlas

Edited by Norman Barrett

PURNELL

MAN AND THE ENVIRONMENT

When people used to talk about the environment, they used to mean the village, town, or region where they lived. Nowadays, by environment we mean the whole Earth. With advances in the study of man and living things in general, it has become apparent that the study of life does not make sense unless considered side by side with the environment in which it develops. The environment exerts influence on life, conditions it, favours or hinders it. These considerations have led to the birth of ecology, the study of the interdependence of living organisms, both animal and vegetable, and the environment. The various environments to be found on Earth may be identified broadly as the sea and the mountains, the forests and the plains, the polar regions and the deserts. Throughout very long periods of evolution, each environment has 'selected' the plants and animals suitable only for that particular environment and for no other, and has created a perfect and delicate balance that only man has seriously disturbed and threatens still. The study of the different environments and of their characteristics must teach us to respect the environment itself and the balance Nature has created over the millions of years of evolution.

THE POLAR REGIONS Although distinguished by their very harsh climate, the polar regions are not without life. The Arctic is a great sea, covered by ice for most of the year, but rich in phytoplankton (tiny floating plants) and full of fish, particularly near the American and Eurasian coasts. In the brief summer period, short grasses, mosses, and lichens grow on the tundra. This habitat attracts many kinds of animals and birds, which come to breed in these remote lands. The Antarctic is a true frozen continent, and has become, in more recent years, an immense laboratory for scientific research.

MOUNTAINS AND FORESTS The mountains, with their poor and eroded soil, harsh climate, and rarefied air, are inhabited by extremely specialized animal and vegetable forms, in perfect balance with each other. Forests of broad-leaved trees extend over the mountainsides at varying altitudes, depending on latitude, degree of exposure, and type of soil. As conditions become less favourable, these are gradually replaced by trees with acicular (needle-shaped) leaves, and then by smaller, stunted trees, giving way to shrubs and then grasses, mosses, and lichens.

THE TROPICAL FOREST Tropical forests offer the most hospitable environment for vegetable and animal life. The constant heat and the rains, which are evenly distributed throughout the year, enable plants to reproduce, flower, and bear fruit without interruption. An enormous variety of animal life at every level of the forest matches the luxurious growth of vegetation (large trees with dense foliage, epiphytes, lianas, and dense undergrowth of tall grasses, ferns, and shrubs). This type of forest prevails in central South America, central Africa, and south-eastern Asia.

GRASSLANDS AND SAVANNAS In general, the grassland is the area that separates forest from desert. It is not wet enough to sustain large trees, but is able to feed a wide variety of grasses. The appearance and features of grassland are determined by the local temperature, the composition of the soil, and the amount of rainfall. The savanna is found in the warm intertropical regions, where a long drought follows a short period of rain. The steppes occur in subtropical regions with a very dry climate or in those continental regions with prolonged droughts.

THE DESERT Plants and animals that inhabit the deserts live by taking and storing what little water there is, water that comes from the sometimes violent but rare rains that fall, sometimes years apart. The great differences in temperature between day and night, together with the loose, rocky or sandy soil, have led to the development of flora and fauna highly adapted to this particular environment. Oases, found where water in the underlying aquifer (the water-bearing layer of rock or sand) approaches the surface, bring about a special development of animal and vegetable life.

THE SEA The sea is the environment in which life began, and it covers 70 per cent of the Earth's surface. Even though it assumes various geographical names, the sea is one intercommunicating whole. It houses a greater variety of life than any other environment on Earth. The basis of life in the sea, as in every other biome (life-zone), is vegetation, and all sea animals feed directly or indirectly on phytoplankton. Different biological areas of the sea can also be distinguished, with differing features and requirements according to depth, temperature, and pressure.

7

EUROPE

Geologists, naturalists, and scholars all find a certain difficulty in defining Europe as a continent in itself. Some say it would be better to speak of *Eurasia,* considering Europe to be almost a huge, highly indented peninsula of Asia, but so closely linked to the main continent as to make it impossible to define its eastern boundary.

It is joined to Asia at the line of the Ural Mountains, in Russia, and the boundary between the two continents then runs south along the River Ural to the Caspian Sea. Between the Caspian Sea and the Black Sea the boundary follows another natural feature, the Caucasus Mountains, which separate Europe from the Middle East region of Asia. The northern mountain chains, in Scotland and Scandinavia, are the oldest. The alpine chains (Pyrenees, Alps, Apennines, Carpathians, Balkans, and Caucasus), running from west to east in southern Europe, go back only to the Tertiary period (50 million years ago), and are therefore among the youngest mountains in the world. After the Tertiary period, Europe experienced at least four ice ages. The last of these ice ages, having lasted nearly 100,000 years, began to retreat only 25,000 years ago. Prehistoric man had already painted his masterpieces in the caves of Lascaux (France) and Altamira (Spain).

The present-day appearance of Europe has therefore been formed by ice in very recent times, and is still being subjected to considerable transformations. The most marked of these are the slow but continuous retreat of the glaciers, the continual transformation of the large deltas (Po, Rhône, and Danube), the intense volcanic activity in certain areas (Iceland and the Apennines), and the powerful action of earthquakes in the south-east (Greece, Yugoslavia, and Italy).

Despite its relatively uniform appearance (Europe has no tropical regions) and the far-reaching intervention of man, the European scene, whether on the sea, in the mountains, or on the plains, is an extremely fascinating one.

Above: A plant of the Vitaceae family, the vine *(Vitis vinifera)* is widely cultivated in many varieties for the production of both wine and dessert grapes. The main centres of cultivation are the Mediterranean region and central-southern Europe. The vine is a plant of temperate climates, although it can adapt to marked variations of temperature. It is cultivated in various ways—headed vines, cordon vines, or trained to canes or trellises. It is propagated by means of cuttings, i.e. by cutting a young branch and planting it in the soil, thereby creating a new plant.

Left: On the Atlantic coast of Ireland, the cliffs of Moher fall sheer into the sea for about 8 km, from a uniform height of over 200 m. Many kinds of birds nest in the ravines.

Above: The Swiss Alps are the most famous part of the Alpine chain. The snow-covered peaks emerge from the clouds, which trace the outline of the valleys beneath, as over the Lake of Lucerne (or Lake of Four Forest Cantons).

Below: Wheat is the general term for various species of the *Triticum* genus of the Gramineae family. The cultivation of wheat goes back to prehistoric times. It is the main source of nourishment of the human race. The flour obtained by milling the grains of wheat is superior to other cereals for nutritive value and taste. The cultivation of wheat is widespread throughout the world, and covers more of the Earth's surface than any other food crop. One of the world's major areas of production is southern and central Europe, particularly the vast Russian plains. Russia grows more wheat than any other country in the world, with nearly 30% of the total produced.

Below: One of the most famous caves in France, Orgnac Cave is in the Massif Central, not far from the Rhône Valley. It is neither the largest nor the deepest cave in France, but it contains some extremely beautiful limestone formations, noted for their delicate shape and splendid colours.

9

EUROPE - PHYSICAL

ALPINE FLORA—GENTIAN

ARBUTUS BERRY (STRAWBERRY TREE)

ALPINE FLORA—EDELWEISS

SUNFLOWER

ALPINE FLORA (see photographs p.11)

This is a general term for a wide variety of plants that grow in mountainous regions and are particularly suited to mountain climate and environment. They are generally short-stemmed to resist strong winds, and have well-developed roots in order to reach water, which is lacking on the surface. They have small, waxy or downy leaves to limit transpiration (giving off of water) and to resist the intense cold. Their vegetative period is very short, corresponding to the intense, but brief, season of summer warmth.

Gentian (*Gentiana*), a plant of the Gentianaceae family, grows on mountains at over 4,000 m above sea level. Some species of gentian are sought after not just for the beautiful deep blue flower, but also for their roots, which are used in medicine.

Edelweiss (*Leontopodium alpinum*), the most famous, perhaps, of Alpine flowers, grows only above 1,500 m, and, because it is so rare, has almost become the symbol of mountaineering. Its name means 'noble white', from the German, and it is the national flower of Switzerland.

BLUE GROTTO

Capri, some 30 km south of Naples, is one of the most beautiful Mediterranean islands. Its rocky white coastline is honeycombed with caves and grottoes, of which the Blue Grotto is the most famous. Owing to the gradual subsidence of the coast, the sun's rays now enter the cave from an opening below the sea, filling it with a hazy blue light and giving a luminous silvery appearance to things below the surface.

CAIRNGORMS NATIONAL NATURE RESERVE

This is the largest nature reserve in Britain, with an area of over 250 sq km. The Cairngorms, with several peaks over 1,200 m, lie in the central highlands of Scotland and are part of the Grampian range. The country is rugged and lonely, offering some of Europe's most striking scenery for the hardy walker. The flora includes Scots pines, birch, and juniper trees and struggling Alpine and Arctic plants. The golden eagle lives in eyries 450 to 600 m up in the mountains, and there are capercaillies and wildcats.

CAMARGUE

The region of the marshy Rhône delta, also called the 'European Wild West'. Near Arles, the Rhône divides into two branches, forming a broad triangle, a real desert of sand and shallow *étangs* (lagoons). The largest is the Étang de Vaccarès, at the centre. La Camargue is a botanical and zoological sanctuary, with poor, but brightly coloured, flora (tamarisks, thistles, short grasses), to which rice and vines have recently been added. The birdlife is very rich and varied, with flamingos, tropical birds, and birds of passage. A major occupation is the extensive breeding of herds of fighting bulls and beautiful white horses.

CASTELLANA GROTTOES

Justifiably described as 'a fantasy in limestone', these caves are in central Apulia, in the 'heel' of Italy, a region of low limestone hills called the *murge*. The most extensive and spectacular cave system in Italy, it was discovered in 1938 and has been cleverly illuminated to bring out the beauty of the coloured alabaster stalactites and stalagmites and the dramatic luminescence of the limestone, which has intensified over thousands of years.

Above: Reindeer of the tundra. In the remote past, the tundra reindeer *(Rangifer tarandus)* were to be found over most of Europe. Now they live in a state of semi-domesticity in northern Europe and Siberia. In the summer, the gentle and docile reindeer gather together in large herds and move on to very high altitudes or wander around on the damp plains, feeding on aromatic herbs, flowers, and young shoots. In winter, they migrate to more southern areas in search of moss and lichen. The reindeer provide an indispensable means of support for the Laplanders. As well as serving as a means of transport, they supply milk, meat, hides, and wool.

Centre: Geological phenomena have gradually broken up the coastline of Iceland, scattering around the island a series of peninsulas and tiny islands, such as the one in the picture, in the Westman Islands (Vestmannaeyjar), off the southern coast. Iceland arose in the form of an island as a result of complex geological events which, in certain aspects, were unique in the world. Millions of years ago, when most of the world's land masses rose from the depths of the sea, this phenomenon in Iceland was accompanied by spectacular volcanic activity that created almost the whole of the present surface.

Left: Geysers represent the most spectacular phenomenon of volcanic origin in Iceland. They consist of 'hver', spouts of steam and water at temperatures of 100°C, and 'laug', warm-water springs. The largest geyser in the world is the Deildartunguhver, north of Reykjavik, which spurts out 250 litres of water per second. The famous Great Geyser, which can be seen in the picture, is shown in a state of much reduced activity.

CHEDDAR GORGE

One of Britain's most dramatic natural phenomena, these towering limestone cliffs lie in the Mendip Hills, in Somerset. Thought to have been cut by a stream now underground, the gorge rises to a height of 137 m and is best seen on descending into the village of Cheddar. Several caves are open to visitors. Cox's Cave and Gough's Cave contain notable stalactites and stalagmites. Old Stone Age tools and weapons were found in Gough's Cave, along with the skeleton of Cheddar Man, who lived there about 12,000 years ago at the end of the Ice Age and whose remains were discovered in 1903.

DANUBE

The second-longest river in Europe, and perhaps the most fascinating in the variety of landscapes through which it flows. Its source is in the Black Forest, and it reaches the Black Sea after flowing for 2,775 km. It crosses as many as six countries (Germany, Austria, Hungary, Yugoslavia, Romania, and Bulgaria), and flows through three capitals—Vienna, Budapest, and Belgrade. The most beautiful stretches of the river are at Passau, in Germany; in Austria, between Linz and Vienna; and on the Yugoslav-Romanian border, at the famous gorge called the Iron Gate. A 1,287-m dam was completed at the Iron Gate in 1972, raising the water level by 35 m to form a gigantic lake, 250 km long.

EELS

It was only in the early 1900s, after many years of study, that the mystery of the life of the eel (*Anguilla anguilla*) was solved. Until then, neither the place of hatching nor the exact method of reproduction was known. Found in nearly all inland waters of Europe, particularly at the mouths of rivers, in pools, and in the marshes of the upper Adriatic, eels reach sexual maturity during their 12th year of life. They then migrate towards the sea, where they undertake long journeys of 3,000-4,000 km to reach an area of the Atlantic Ocean near the West Indies known as the Sargasso Sea. All the eels of Europe, as well as those from the inland waters of North America, migrate there to breed. The larvae, called *leptocephali,* which look like small transparent leaves, slowly develop and then allow the Gulf Stream to carry them back towards their respective native waters. About three years after hatching, the young eels, called *elvers* at this stage, arrive at the mouths of rivers. They swim upstream in serried ranks of millions to reach the ponds and marshes, where they will complete their development and, on reaching sexual maturity, will undertake a new reproductive migration.

EURIPUS CHANNEL

A strait, only 39 m wide, between the Greek mainland and the island of Euboea (Évvoia), in the Aegean Sea. Today it is crossed by a swing bridge, facing the city of Chalcis (Khalkis), 56 km north of Athens. In this narrow strait, a curious phenomenon occurs that has been studied for thousands of years and is still not well understood. The very strong and dangerous current reverses direction a dozen times a day, making navigation possible only in that particular direction.

FIGHTING BULLS

Until a few years ago, herds of bulls were bred in a semi-wild state on the plains of the Camargue (a marshy and uncultivated area at the mouth of the Rhône, in France) and in Andalusia (Spain) for bullfighting. Nowadays, fighting bulls are selected by careful breeding to produce the required characteristics of strength, speed, and ferocity. The sport is practised in Spain and to a lesser extent in Portugal and southern France.

FIGS

The fig tree (*Ficus carica*) is a plant of the mulberry family (Moraceae), cultivated in the Mediterranean region (Italy, Spain, Portugal, Turkey, and Albania) for its fruit (figs), which are eaten fresh or dry, or used in the preparation of sweetmeats, fermented drinks, syrups, and jams. Because cultivated figs have only female flowers, fertilization is induced by a method called 'caprification'. This consists of hanging a flowering branch of the wild fig, or caprifig, in the cultivated fig tree, so that the pollen from the caprifig fertilizes the cultivated fig. Pollination occurs thanks to the tiny fig wasp, which completes its life-cycle in the wild fig tree. Figs are mentioned in the Bible, and were greatly appreciated by the ancient Egyptians, Greeks, and Romans.

The archipelago of Svalbard, or the Spitsbergen Islands, situated midway between Norway (to which they belong) and the North Pole, are among the most interesting lands of the Arctic. Fossilized remains of tropical animals have been found there, testifying to the fact that the islands enjoyed a very hot climate during the Tertiary period.

The Siberian taiga lies just south of the tundra. It is a vast belt of coniferous trees, the largest forest in the world, including firs, spruces, larches, and pines. There are also some deciduous trees (poplars, alders, birches). It is the realm of bears, sables, and pine martens. The taiga is marshy in places and the trees there are rotten. But timber is exploited, and transported along the rivers, such as the Yenisey. There are also rich mineral deposits (coal, iron, gold), and animals are trapped for their furs.

A feature typical of Scotland, the lochs (lakes) lie in hollows formed by glaciation or by moraines left by retreating glaciers. The smaller lochs are called *tarns*; the larger, *glen*, lochs lie in long hollows in the glens. The longest is Loch Ness, which is 39 km long, 1.5 km wide, 230 m deep, and never freezes. The biggest is Loch Lomond, which is not quite as long as Loch Ness, but has an area of 70 sq km. The lake in the photograph is Loch Uisge, in the west of Scotland.

A fossil fuel, peat is partly decayed plant matter that has collected in marshes and swamps over a long period of time. It forms in layers, and is generally the first stage in the formation of coal. It takes the form of spongy lumps, varying from yellow-brown (like tangled hay) to the dark brown lower layers, which contain 90 per cent water. Peat bogs are found in a number of countries of northern Europe, including Russia, Finland, Ireland (see photograph, *below*), the Netherlands, and Germany.

FIORDS
Norway is an enormous mountainous massif. In very ancient times it was subjected to violent upheavals and fractures, until it stabilized with a gentle slope towards the east and a fractured, very steep part towards the west. In ancient Norwegian, *fjord* (fiord) means a pass or passage. Originally, the fiords were river valleys that were occupied by ice, which, with its weight, lowered the valleys themselves. When the great glaciers melted, the valleys were invaded by the sea. The 'land of fiords' begins north of Stavanger. Some are actual sea straits—the Sògne Fiord is 185 km long, and the Hardanger Fiord is 183 km long. Most fiords have steep rocky walls, with numerous waterfalls rushing down. The scenery is enchanting, with thick woods, and sometimes small areas of fertile farmland below the cliffs.

FIR
Various species of conifers of the pine family (Pinaceae) are known as fir trees, and these include the pines (genus *Pinus*) and the spruces (genus *Picea*) as well as the true firs (genus *Abies*). The best known of these are the European silver fir (*Abies alba*) and the Norway spruce (*Picea abies*). The European silver fir is a mountain tree with a grey bark, and it forms vast forests on the Alps and the Apennines, the Pyrenees and the Vosges, between 1,000 and 2,000 m above sea level. The Norway spruce (which has a reddish bark) is more resistant to cold than the European silver fir, and forms dense forests on the Alps, the Apennines, and all the mountains of central Europe, Scandinavia, and Russia.

GIANT'S CAUSEWAY
The remarkable Giant's Causeway stretches for 9.5 km along the north coast of County Antrim, in Northern Ireland. It is a striking formation of blocks of basalt thrown up by a submerged volcano in ancient times. The blocks assumed a polygon shape as they fell, overlapping each other to form a gigantic staircase, an amphitheatre of some 40,000 columns. Some are as much as 6 m high, and they are 40–50 cm in diameter. The formation gets its name from an ancient legend that tells of the giant Fin MacCool, who is supposed to have built it to bridge the sea between Ireland and Scotland.

GRAN PARADISO NATIONAL PARK
This was the first Italian national park, and was created in 1922 when King Victor Emmanuel III donated the former hunting lands of the Savoy family to the state. It is a majestic mountainous massif, situated between the valleys of Aosta and Orca, mostly covered by ice. The highest peak is 4,061 m above sea level. Apart from the climbing that can be done there, the Gran Paradiso is famous for its flourishing population of chamois and ibex.

GREAT GLEN OF ALBAN (Glen More)
A valley nearly 100 km long, the Great Glen is a fissure that divides the south-east of Scotland from the north-west. It is navigable by fishing boats and pleasure steamers along a series of lochs (Linnhe, Lochy, Oich, and Ness) connected by 35 km of canal, the whole being known as the Caledonian Canal system. The south-west end of the glen is dominated by the towering granite mass of Ben Nevis, at 1,343 m, the highest peak in the British Isles.

GROSSGLOCKNER
The 'Great Bell-Ringer', 3,797 m above sea level, is the highest peak in the Austrian Alps, and is in the Hohe Tauern range. It is a sharp pyramid, emerging from a mighty group of peaks interspersed with glaciers, among which is the spectacular Pasterze Glacier, 10 km long and 1 km wide. The pass at the foot of the giant mountain can be crossed by car and is 2,981 m above sea level.

HOLLY
An evergreen shrub or small tree of the Aquifoliaceae family, the holly (*Ilex aquifolium*) has beautiful shiny, leathery, and prickly leaves, and bright-red fruits in berry form. It grows wild in woods below mountain level in most of southern Europe, spreading east across Asia. It is cultivated as an ornamental plant for use particularly at Christmastime.

After the Norway spruce, the larch (*Larix decidua*) is the most abundant coniferous tree in the Alps, where it grows wild between 1,000 and 2,000 m above sea level. It belongs to the pine (Pinaceae) family. It has a straight trunk, conical crown, and thin, needle-shaped deciduous leaves. Reddish-brown cones grow on some of the buds. Its wood is hard and heavy, and is used for floors, door and window frames, posts, and in carpentry.

HOLM OAK

A Mediterranean tree of the beech family (Fagaceae), the holm oak (*Quercus ilex*) has a sturdy trunk with smooth bark, dense foliage, and oval or lanceolate (tapering towards both ends) leaves, which last three or four years. It is a dominant forest tree, sometimes forming whole woods, or growing alongside other trees, such as the maritime pine. It is more frequently found in the western and central Mediterranean (Spain, Italy, Greece, and Yugoslavia). It has a hard, heavy wood, the quality of which is too poor for carpentry, but is excellent as fuel.

ICELANDIC GLACIERS AND VOLCANOES

Iceland is a land of eternal snows and fire—the island itself is formed from volcanic material. Steaming hot springs called *geysers* and erupting volcanoes share the land with glaciers and ice sheets. There are many glaciers, scattered over the entire island, the biggest of which is the Vatnajökull, in the south-east. It is the largest glacier in Europe, with an area of 8,400 sq km and a thickness of up to 1,000 m. It ends at the sea in a vast bed of sand and gravel, interspersed with hundreds of ever-shifting rivulets. About 150 volcanoes date from the period following the Ice Age, and 30 have appeared since records have been kept. The best known is Mt Hekla (1,447 m), in the south, which has erupted several times. In 1963, an underwater volcano rose out of the sea off the south coast, forming an island, now called Surtsey. The Laki Volcano, south-west of the Vatnajökull Glacier, has 100 craters within a distance of 25 km. Its eruption in 1783 lasted six months, and the lava output of 563 sq km was the most impressive in history.

JUNGFRAU

The most famous mountain in Switzerland, and one of the most dramatic in the Alps, it reaches a height of 4,158 m, and is covered in huge glaciers, which unite to form the Aletsch Glacier, one of the principal glaciers of the Alpine chain. This beautiful mountain is easily reached by a rack railway, which goes as high as 3,454 m to the edge of the Aletsch Glacier. From this point, the peak may be reached with the aid of specialist guides.

JUNIPER

A shrub, or small tree, of the cypress family (Cupressaceae), the juniper (*Juniperus communis*) is widespread throughout Europe and

North America. In Europe there is a dwarf variety, suited to the cold climate of high mountain regions, which can exist, exposed to the wind, in the most barren soil—it can be found even at 3,700 m above sea level on the Monte Rosa mountains. The juniper has acicular (needlelike) leaves and fleshy blue-black berrylike fruits, or cones. The fruits contain an oil used in making gin and to flavour some other alcoholic drinks, and for certain medicinal preparations.

LAPLAND

The extreme northern region of Europe is a bleak, barren area stretching across Norway, Sweden, Finland, and part of Russia. It is called Lapland because it is inhabited by a small, hardy people called Lapps. Lapland covers an area of about 400,000 sq km. During the Ice Age, the ground was covered with a layer of ice several kilometres thick. The melting of the ice produced several phenomena: uplifting of the ground (a metre

An imposing crystalline massif with 10 peaks, Monte Rosa rises in the Pennine Alps, on the Switzerland–Italy border, and is the second-highest peak in Europe (4,633 m). Huge glaciers descend the mountain and are particularly impressive on the Swiss side. In the photograph are the Belvedere Glacier and the Nordend peak, which is 4,612 m above sea level.

The ibex *(Capra ibex)* is the lord of the alpine peaks. It manages to climb where no other animal dares to tread, because of the shape of its hooves and its fine sense of balance. Indiscriminate hunting in past centuries brought the species to the verge of extinction. Today, the ibex survives, rigorously protected, in the Gran Paradiso National Park in Italy, and in a few animal colonies in Switzerland and Austria.

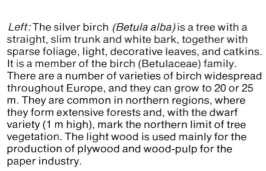

Left: The silver birch *(Betula alba)* is a tree with a straight, slim trunk and white bark, together with sparse foliage, light, decorative leaves, and catkins. It is a member of the birch (Betulaceae) family. There are a number of varieties of birch widespread throughout Europe, and they can grow to 20 or 25 m. They are common in northern regions, where they form extensive forests and, with the dwarf variety (1 m high), mark the northern limit of tree vegetation. The light wood is used mainly for the production of plywood and wood-pulp for the paper industry.

15

Considered to be among the most beautiful mountains in the world, the Dolomites occupy a large area of the regions of Trentino–Alto Adige and Veneto, in north-eastern Italy. They have a fascinating geological history. Dolomite is a limestone that has risen from the sea bed, and is therefore encrusted with thousands upon thousands of marine fossils. The action of sea and wind has formed spectacular crags and towers of rock, which are streaked with dazzling colours owing to the presence of various minerals. One of the most famous places in the Dolomites is Lake Misurina *(above)*, which is set amidst wonderful fir woods and huge walls of rock, from which rise the Tre Cime di Lavaredo (2,999 m).

each century), where it was no longer weighed down by ice; and the formation of morainic hills and alluvial deposits. On the north coast, the climate is rather mild in the 3-month summer (14°C), while inland the winter (9 months) is very harsh, temperatures dropping as low as −50°C. Under the snow, the soil freezes from November to May. Flora is limited to lichen, mosses, and dwarf trees (birch, pine, and fir). The fauna is represented by reindeer, which serve as draft and pack animals and also as a source of food.

LAUREL
A small evergreen tree or shrub, typical of the Mediterranean scrub, the laurel (*Laurus nobilis*) belongs to the Lauraceae family. It has leathery leaves with crinkled margins and black aromatic fruits in drupe form, from which an oil is extracted for use in the manufacture of soap and perfume. Also cal-

led bay, or Grecian, laurel, it is cultivated as an ornamental plant, particularly for garden hedges. In ancient times, the brows of poets and victorious generals or athletes were decorated with laurel leaves. Today it is a symbol of academic distinction. Plants of some other families are also called laurels, such as the cherry laurel, which is not a true laurel, but a member of the rose family.

LOCH NESS
A long, narrow lake in northern Scotland, Loch Ness is famous for its fauna—namely, the 'Loch Ness Monster', a creature claimed to have been seen by many and which has appeared in all shapes and sizes, but never clearly, in photographs, but whose existence has never been proved. Regular reports of a monster in the loch date back to the 1200s, and were revived in the 1930s. Sophisticated scientific methods have been used to plumb the depths of the loch from end to end in search of evidence of 'Nessie', as the phenomenon has become affectionately known. And thousands of tourists flock to the loch sides every year, not just for the beautiful scenery, but to indulge in the rapidly growing sport of 'monster spotting'.

MATTERHORN
This is called simply 'the Mountain', as it is the very epitome of a mountain, both for its isolated position and for its dramatic pyramidal shape. It reaches a height of 4,478 m, and among its rocks there are numerous glaciers. At its foot, there is a station for the study of solar radiation. The conquest of the Matterhorn is one of the most fascinating stories in the history of mountaineering. The peak was first reached on 14 July 1865, by Edward Whymper, an Englishman, who climbed up from the Swiss side; four of his party fell to their deaths on the descent. Three days later an Italian party, led by J. A. Carrel, arrived from the Italian side.

MONT BLANC
The most impressive massif of the Alpine chain, Mont Blanc is an enormous block of crystalline schists, covered to a great extent with ice, and reaching an altitude of 4,810 m, the highest point in Europe (excluding the Caucasus). It is nearly 50 km long and 15 km wide. A great attraction of the massif is the possibility of crossing it by cable-car, along the most daring rope railway in Europe: from Entrèves, in Italy, the cableway audaciously crosses the glacier called Mer de Glace (Sea of Ice), and reaches the Helbronner Peak at 3,452 m above sea level; from there, a tunnel dug through the ice leads into French territory, just below the peak of the Aiguille du Midi (3,843 m), which can be reached by a lift. Another almost vertical cableway descends from the Aiguille du Midi to Chamonix, the great Alpine resort bordered by the glaciers that descend from Mont Blanc.

OLYMPUS
This most famous, isolated, and arid mountain of classical times, the mythical dwelling-place of the gods, lies on the eastern edge of the ridge that separates Thessaly and Macedonia, in Greece. The lower slopes of Olympus, between 1,200 and 1,600 m above sea level, are covered in woods and are easily accessible. The higher slopes consist of the wild valley of Mavrolongos, which is encircled by the various peaks. Its summit, which is 2,911 m above sea level, is the highest peak in Greece. It is difficult to climb, and special guides and equipment are necessary.

One of the most picturesque parts of the Côte d'Azur, in southern France, Esterel is a forested region between Fréjus and Cannes. Walls of red rocks surrounding tiny bays rise sheer from the sea all along the coast, and pine trees, which grow to the very edge of the sea, add a vivacious splash of green to the red of the rocks and the blue of the sea.

POLDERS

Cultivated lands obtained by reclamation from the sea and protected by structures such as dykes and dams, polders are to be found all over Europe, but nowhere in such large numbers or obtained at the cost of so much persistent and patient work as in the Netherlands. There, the large rivers that flow into the North Sea (Schelde, Maas, and Waal) have built weak barriers of dunes, behind which depressions, on average 6–7 m below sea level, have formed. The battle against the sea has lasted for centuries, with fluctuating fortunes: in 1931, the gigantic Zuiderzee Dam enabled 1,600 sq km to be won from the sea, but in 1953, on the other hand, the sea swallowed up the Zeeland islands. At present, work is under way on the Delta Project, scheduled to be completed in the early 1980s. This provides for the construction of enclosure dams in the estuaries between the islands in the south-western part of the country and the creation of freshwater reservoirs.

POSTOJNA CAVES

On the limestone plateau of the Karst in Yugoslavia, there are numerous examples of underground erosion. The most prominent of these are the Postojna Caves, in the north-west. One of the country's most remarkable sights, the caves extend over a vast area, spreading out into a labyrinth of hundreds of kilometres of passageways and potholes. During the war, the Germans used them as a fuel dump, but Partisans discovered an uncharted entrance and blew up 10,000 tonnes of petrol. Only eight of the caves may be visited, of which five are linked by a small electric train. The huge caverns and grottoes are lined with spectacular stalagmites and stalactites—concrete phantoms, illusions of castles and skyscrapers, cloisters and minarets. A cavern 35 m high, called the Concert Hall, is reached on foot. It holds 10,000 people, and symphony concerts are staged there. In a pool in the nearby Crystal Hall lives a strange eyeless creature, *Proteus anguineus*, a living fossil that is found nowhere else. Palish white and pink and 20-30 cm long, they are strangely grotesque, with limbs bearing a marked resemblance to human hands and feet—they have been described as looking like 'peeled lizards'.

A tree of the Oleaceae family, the olive *(Olea europaea)* originated in Asia Minor, and is now found in the Mediterranean area (Spain, Italy, southern France, Greece, and Tunisia). In its wild state, it is a large bush, with many stems growing out of the main trunk, but when cultivated it has a tree-like appearance, with a contorted trunk and elevated, horizontal branches. It lives a very long time, and is cultivated for its fruit, the olive *(right)*, which has a fleshy pulp and from which oil is obtained. The olive tree begins to produce fruit during its ninth or tenth year. Productivity then increases until the tree is 35–45 years old, and tails off between the age of 50 and 100 years. The main producers of olive oil are Italy and Spain.

RHINE

The river that symbolizes German history and tradition to the point of being called 'der Vater Rhein' (Father Rhine) by the Germans. It flows for 1,320 km and drains an area of about 200,000 sq km. The Rhine proper begins near Chur, in Switzerland, at the confluence of the Hinterrhein and the Vorderrhein, two glacier-fed mountain torrents that issue at heights of 2,216 m and 2,344 m, respectively. It flows along the Swiss borders with Liechtenstein and Austria into Lake Constance, nearly 400 m above sea level, and then past Schaffhausen to form the famous Rhine Falls, with a drop of 21 m. After Basel, the Rhine is navigable for 740 km, and interesting cruises can be made along it, with the Vosges Mountains (France) to the west and Germany's Black Forest to the east. The Rhine Valley in Germany has some marvellous scenery, and as the river leaves the plain at Bingen it plunges into a narrow gorge, and past the Lorelei, a rock where, according to legend, the water nymph Lorelei used to lure sailors to destruction. In its final section, in the Netherlands, the Rhine splits into a broad delta before flowing into the North Sea.

Oaks are evergreen trees of the beech (Fagaceae) family. The cork oak *(Quercus suber)* is a majestic tree, widespread throughout the central and western Mediterranean region, particularly in Portugal and Spain. It is cultivated for its cork bark, which can be as thick as 15 cm. The first stripping, undertaken when the tree is between 16 and 20 years old, produces virgin cork, which is inelastic. From successive strippings, 10–14 years apart, a better, elastic cork is obtained. Cork has many uses, such as insulation, gaskets, and bottle-stoppers.

Above: Mediterranean scrub. This type of vegetation is characteristic of the Mediterranean region, where the summers are hot and dry and the winters mild with heavy rains. It is a dense evergreen brushwood, sometimes reaching a height of 3–5 m, made up of shrubs and small trees, with sparsely scattered tall trees. The Mediterranean scrub consists mainly of arbute, heather, juniper, laurel, lentisk, oleander, myrtle, honeysuckle, and rosemary.

Below: An imposing tree of the beech (Fagaceae) family, the sweet chestnut *(Castanea sativa)* forms extensive woods below the 800 m level in the countries bordering the northern Mediterranean (Italy, France, Spain, and the Balkan Peninsula). The undergrowth around this majestic tree harbours a rich flora of shrubs (juniper, heather, and strawberry) and grasses. The sweet chestnut, commonly called simply the 'chestnut', is economically very important, both for its strong, solid wood and for its fruits. The wood is used in the construction industry, in making barrels and furniture, and in the production of tannin for the tanning industry. The fruits are edible nuts (chestnuts), which develop from the female flowers.

SEVERN BORE
The Severn is the longest river in Britain, rising in central Wales and flowing about 350 km to the Bristol Channel. Because of its funnel-shaped estuary, the river is subjected to a high bore (a kind of tidal wave) several times a year. It rushes up the river at about 20 km/h, reaching a height of nearly 3 m and sometimes causing extensive flooding. Sportsmen have taken advantage of this phenomenon to create world-record surfing rides of over 6 km.

SNOWDONIA
This, the most beautiful and famous of national parks in Britain, stretches across north-western Wales. It is a region of wild mountains, all about 1,000 m above sea level, completely bare and devoid of vegetation, reflected in quaint little lakes. An 8-km-long narrow-gauge, rack-and-pinion railway climbs the peak of Mt Snowdon from the village of Llanberis. Snowdon, at 1,085 m above sea level, is the highest peak in England and Wales, and is a beautiful mountain of porphyry and slate, with a summit that splits into five precipitous peaks. Some rare flora and fauna are to be found in the National Park, including the Snowdon lily and the gwyniad *(Coregonus pennanti),* a whitefish about 25 cm long, found only in Bala Lake, in the east of Snowdonia.

Right: A herbaceous plant of the Chenopodiaceae family, sugar-beet *(Beta vulgaris)* is widely cultivated in Germany, Poland, Czechoslovakia, and the USSR for its fleshy root, which contains 13-22 per cent sugar. Its cultivation as a vegetable, which goes back to ancient times, gained importance in 1749, when a German scientist, Andreas Marggraf, first extracted sugar from it. The beets are washed and sliced and left in warm water to soak. After several stages of straining, a syrup is obtained which is filtered and condensed to separate the raw sugar, and this is then refined. The pulp (the remains of the beet slices) is used as animal feed.

STAFFA
In the group of islands called the Inner Hebrides, off the west coast of Scotland, near the island of Mull, rises Staffa. This is an uninhabited island of basalt, only 2.5 km in circumference, and is one of the most beautiful of these products of the violent volcanic explosions that took place millions of years ago. The columnar formations and caves are fantastic. The most famous is Fingal's Cave, 69 m long with an entrance 20 m high, which is mentioned in romantic literature and which inspired Mendelssohn to compose *The Hebrides* overture, also called *Fingal's Cave.* The floors, walls, and roof of the cave are made of black pentagonal or hexagonal pillars of basaltic rock. Steamers from Oban, on the mainland, visit Staffa, and landings may be made in calm seas. About 10 km to the south lies the historic island of Iona.

STRAWBERRY TREE (see photograph p.11)
A species *(Arbutus unedo)* of *Arbutus,* evergreen shrubs or small trees of the Ericaceae (heather) family. It has shiny, leathery leaves, clusters of whitish flowers, and berry-type fruits that are red when ripe and look like strawberries. It grows in northern France, south-western Ireland, and Mediterranean lands.

STROMBOLI
Stromboli, the most northerly of the Lipari Islands (north of Sicily), has an area of only 12 sq km. Its volcano is famous both for its height of 926 m and for the spectacular display of its continuous explosions. The climb is always undertaken at night because of the brilliant illuminations emanating from the crater. The most enchanting point is Sciara del Fuoco (best visible from the sea), where the lava, cinders, and lapilli (small fragments) can be seen descending the sides of the volcano in an incandescent state, and hurtling into the sea with an infernal din of rumbling and hissing steam along a front about a kilometre long.

SUNFLOWER (see photograph p.11)
A herbaceous plant of the Compositae family, the sunflower *(Helianthus annuus)* originated in America. Special varieties are widely cultivated for grain and oil in Russia and Hungary. Its stem can be 2–3 m tall, its leaves are heart-shaped, and it has large, gaudy blooms with diameters as much as 50 cm. An edible oil is

extracted from the seeds for use in cooking, and in the production of margarine, soaps, and paints. The seeds of the grain variety, roasted and pressed into cakes, are used for cattle- and chicken-feed.

TUNNY

The tunny belongs to the Scombridae family, a group of fish that also includes mackerel. The tunny, or bluefin tuna *(Thunnus thynnus)*, the largest species, may be more than 3 m long and weigh 500 kg. It is widespread in the eastern Atlantic and the Mediterranean. An impressive swimmer, the tunny is capable of making long migrations. At breeding time, tunny migrate to their Mediterranean spawning grounds in shoals, and fishermen take advantage of this habit. Tunny are among the world's most important food fish, rich in vitamins and protein. France and Spain are the leading tunny-fishing countries in Europe.

VALLEY OF THE BUTTERFLIES

This is certainly the most visited place on the much visited island of Rhodes, and one of the most romantic places in Europe. The beautiful little valley, in the shade of pines and chestnut trees, refreshed by the waters of little brooks, is just 25 km from the city of Rhodes, near the ancient town of Kamiros. In the summer months, the valley fills with millions of beautiful butterflies, a thrilling sight when they are stirred up into deep red clouds.

VESUVIUS

This is the best-known volcano in the world, because of the numerous views of Naples showing the characteristic shape of Vesuvius. It is the only active volcano on the mainland of Europe, and is as active now as in ancient times. Its eruptions have caused many disasters, such as the destruction of Pompeii and Herculaneum in AD 79, Torre del Greco in 1872, and San Sebastiano in 1944. Several towns were devastated in 1906, in an eruption that literally took the top off Vesuvius—from a height of 1,303 m to 1,171 m. A chair-lift goes up to the Vesuvius Observatory, which was constructed in 1845 at 609 m above sea level. Another chair-lift goes from 754 m to 1,158 m, right up to the edge of the crater. Accompanied by a guide, one can look over the edge of the cone down into the abyss. In normal times, Vesuvius spouts columns of steam, cinders, and occasionally small amounts of lava. The panorama of the gulfs of Naples and Gaeta, and of the famous Neapolitan islands is incomparable. The slopes of the volcano, where the soil is extremely fertile, are famous for their vineyards. Many people live on the lower slopes and at the foot of the mountain despite its history of eruptions.

WISENT

Very widespread during the Pleistocene period, from Russia to the plain of the Po and the Pyrenees (as evidenced by the cave art found in certain parts of France and at Altamira, in Spain), the wisent, or European bison *(Bison bonasus),* has now been reduced to a few dozen specimens surviving in the forest of Bialowicz, in Poland. It belongs to the same genus as the American bison, and is the biggest of European land mammals. Agile, despite its size, it would defend itself from the attacks of bears and wolves by charging or fleeing. It could not, however, withstand the more deadly attack represented by man's hunting activities. The hunt organized on Bialowicz Heath in 1752 has remained tragically famous: 2,000 beaters were employed to drive hundreds of wisent to their deaths.

Standing on the eastern coast of Sicily, Mount Etna is the highest volcano in Europe and one of the most active in the world. The huge cone has a perimeter of about 160 km at its base, and rises to a height of 3,296 m. It is covered with a mantle of snow during most of the year, and, in contrast to the flourishing belt of vines, olives, and orange groves spread out at its base, only lichens grow at its highest levels. Its fertile slopes are the most thickly populated area of Sicily. Since records have been kept, over a hundred eruptions have taken place, some of which have been disastrous. The city of Catania was destroyed in 1169 and again in 1669, when an accompanying earthquake killed some 20,000 people. In the photograph *(right)* of the 1971 eruption, the escape of ash, lava, and lapilli (small fragments) can be clearly seen. A road leads from Catania to the Sapienza mountain refuge, at 1,910 m above sea level. From this point, a cableway goes up to the observatory at 2,915 m. The climb to the crater is quite easy from the observatory.

WOOKEY HOLE

A group of caves worn in the Mendip Hills of Somerset, England, by the River Axe over a period of about 50,000 years, Wookey Hole has provided rich finds of our forebears. It is a complex of limestone caves and grottoes, the first three of which are floodlit and open to visitors. Several others have been explored by cave-divers, the only people equipped to follow the Axe along the submerged passages. There are fantastic shapes to be seen in the caves, including the 'Witch of Wookey', a huge stalagmite. Finds from the caves, human and animal remains of 2,000 years ago, are exhibited in the local museum.

YEW

A conifer of the yew family (Taxaceae), the English yew *(Taxus baccata)* is widespread over Europe, where it grows wild on hills and mountains, about 12 m high and always isolated amidst other tree groups. A tree or shrub, the yew has rich foliage, dark-reddish flaking bark, and linear, evergreen leaves. It grows attractive scarlet berries in the autumn. The seeds, leaves, and branches are poisonous. Yews live for a very long time (up to 2,000 years) and are cultivated in various varieties as ornamental garden plants. They can be pruned to espalier, pyramid, and other shapes. The solid, heavy wood is resistant to damp and is used for decorative veneers and for fence or gate posts. The English archers of the Middle Ages used longbows made of yew wood.

Right: The Meteora are gigantic, almost vertical, spikes of rock, about 300 m high, in central Greece, near Kalabaka, on which Greek monks, with incredible daring, built seven monasteries (1300s–1500s). Steps were cut in the rocks to provide access, and baskets were hauled up by ropes. In the background is the harsh wall of the Pindus Mountains.

ASIA

Above: The highest mountain in the world, Everest is part of the Himalaya range, on the border of Nepal and Tibet. It was named in 1855 in honour of Sir George Everest, the British surveyor-general of India. It was first measured in 1852, when its height was officially recorded as 8,840 m. The present official height is 8,848 m, recorded by an Indian government survey in 1954, but an unofficial height of 8,882 m is also widely quoted. The peak was first conquered on 29 May 1953 by the New Zealander Edmund Hillary and the Nepalese Sherpa Tenzing Norgay, members of the British expedition led by Sir John Hunt. It has since been climbed several times. The Tibetans call the mountain 'Chomolungma', the Nepalese 'Sagarmatha'. Many claim to have seen evidence of a monster they call the 'Yeti', or 'Abominable Snowman', on the mountain, but searches for such a creature have always proved fruitless.

The banyan *(Ficus bengalensis),* a member of the mulberry (Moraceae) family, is native to India and Sri Lanka. It is characterized by its many aerial roots, which grow from seeds dropped into branches by birds. These roots enable it to spread to such an extent that a single tree can form a small dark wood, with foliage 500 m in circumference and hundreds of trunks.

The principal features of Asia may be appreciated by just one look at a map of the world. Most obviously, it is the largest of the continents (45 million sq km). It is also the most central, being like a huge spreading tree, with branches thrusting out towards other land masses. It stretches out in the east almost to touch North America across the Bering Strait. To the west, it is joined to Europe, which is regarded by many geographers as a peninsula of Asia rather than as a separate continent. In the south-west, it touches Africa at the Sinai Peninsula. And the islands of south-eastern Asia spread out towards Australia.

The map also shows three large geographically distinguishable areas that stretch across the continent from west to east. The first, to the north, is Siberia, a vast lowland region. This is *tundra* (treeless, moss-covered marshland) near the Arctic coast, merging into pine and fir forests (*taiga*) and then grasslands called *steppes.* Secondly, there is the central area, created by great folding which lifted from the sea the huge mountain systems of the Hindu Kush, the Karakoram, and the Himalaya. Thirdly, there is the area consisting of the great peninsulas of the Indian Ocean—Arabia, India, and Indochina, which share some of the features of Africa and Australia.

Another feature of Asia is the great variety of climate, from the polar climate of the Arctic coast to the tropical climate of the south. It contains both the coldest inhabited place in the world (−71.1°C has been recorded at Oymyakon, in Siberia) and some of the hottest. The presence of the great wall of mountains at a relatively short distance from the sea causes heavy rainfall in the peninsular fringe and dry conditions in the rest of the continent. Cherrapunji, in northern India, has the highest rainfall in the world, with 26,461 mm in one 12-month period. But the plateau and high mountains of central Asia are so cold and dry that much of the region is desert.

Rice *(Oryza sativa)* is the most important food cereal in Asia, forming the almost exclusive source of nourishment for over half of mankind. It belongs to the grass (Gramineae) family, and grows in tropical and subtropical regions. Indigenous to southern Asia and cultivated in China for thousands of years, rice was introduced into Spain by the Moors in the AD 700s. The Spaniards took rice to Italy in the 1400s and to Latin America in the 1600s. There are thousands of varieties of rice, which can be classified broadly into three groups: mountain rice, cultivated on dry land; paddyfield rice, or rice for cultivation on irrigated land; and glutinous rice (having a high dextrin content). The first and last are used in the Far East for making 'sake' (rice wine) and 'arrack' (rice brandy). Rice is the richest of the cereals in starch content (over 80%) but the poorest in protein (8%). But the quality of the protein is superior to that of wheat. Rice is easily digested and well assimilated. The major producers are China and India.

The largest of the big cats alive today, the tiger *(Panthera tigris)*, is an object of superstition and legends among the populations that fear its ferocity and admire its strength and arrogant beauty. Although widespread in Asia, from Iran to India, in many varieties and greatly differing environments, the tiger prefers the jungle with streams, near which it lies in wait for the antelope, deer, buffalo, and wild boar that go there to drink. Endowed with very acute hearing and exceptional strength and agility, the tiger attacks its prey in a flash, seizing it by the neck, which it breaks, and then tearing the creature apart with its formidable teeth. It attacks man only if wounded or famished.

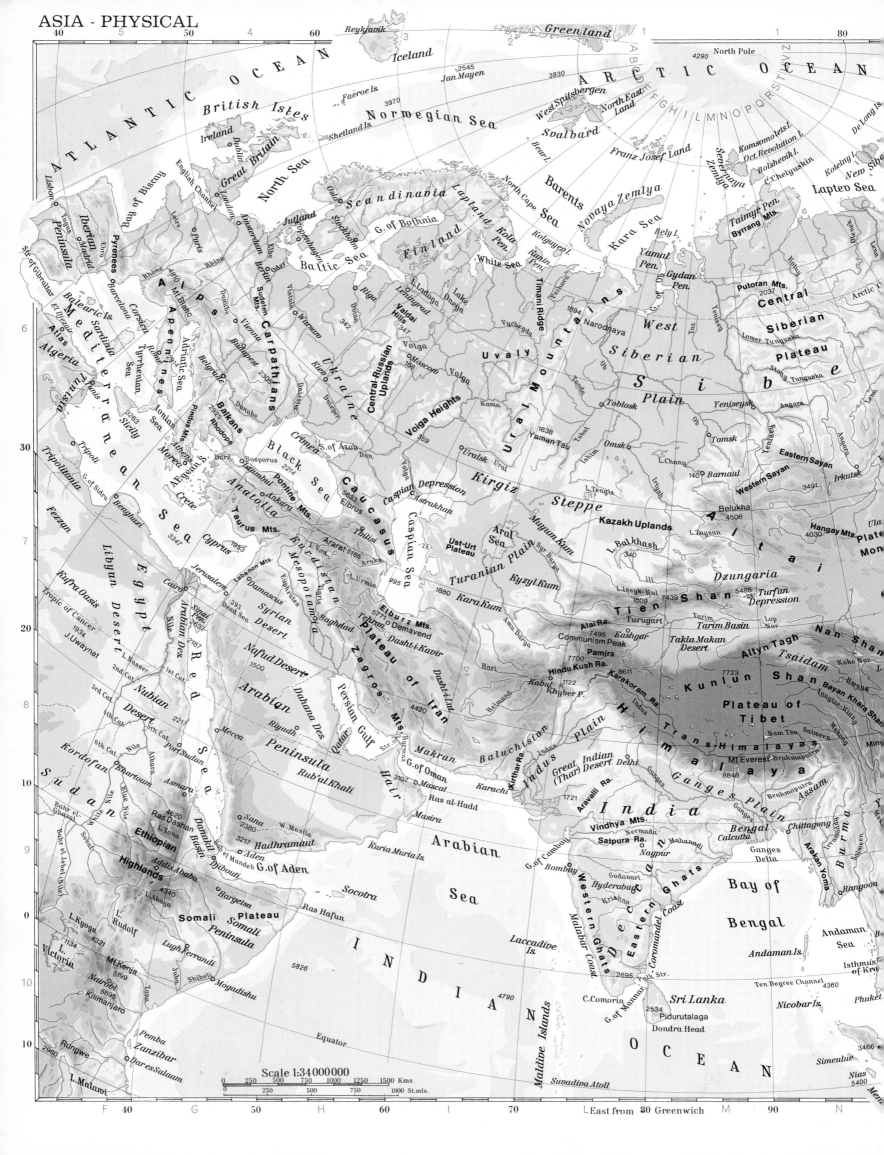

Scale 1:34 000 000

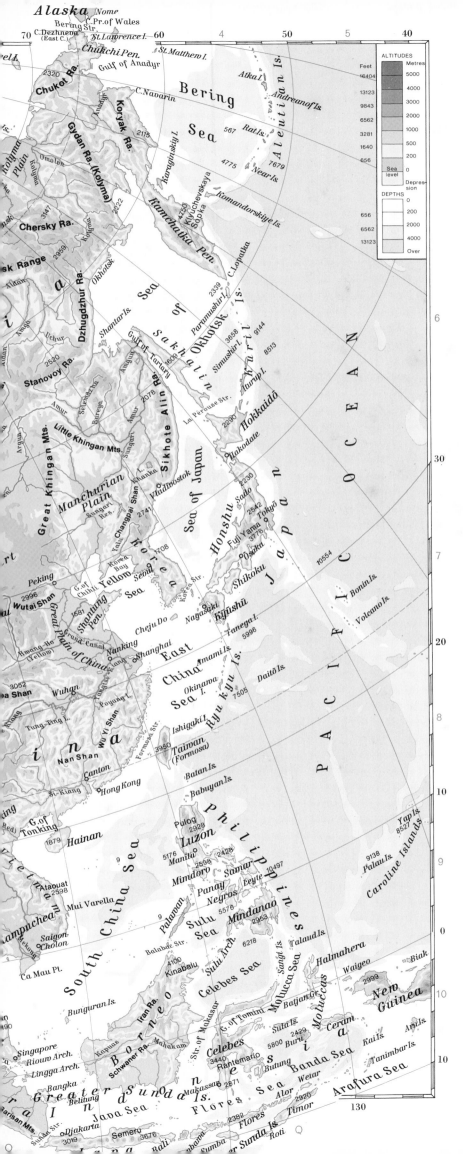

Alaska Nome
Bering C.Pr.of Wales
C.Dezhneva St.Lawrence I.
(East C.)
Chukchi Pen.
Gulf of Anadyr
Chukot Ra.
Koryak Ra.
Gydan Ra. (Kolyma)
Kolyma Plain
Kolyma
Omolon
Chersky Ra.
sk Range
Altan
Dzhugdzhur Ra.
Okhotsk
Stanovoy Ra.
Amur
Little Khingan Mts.
Great Khingan Mts.
Manchurian Plain
Shantar Is.
Sea of Okhotsk
Sakhalin
Gulf of Tartary
Sikhote Alin Ra.
Sungari
Sungari Res.
Changpai Shan
Vladivostok
Khanka L.
Korea Bay
Seoul
Korea Str.
Sea of Japan
Hokkaidō
Hakodate
Honshu
Sado
Fuji Yama
Tokyo
Ōsaka
Shikoku
Kyūshū
Nagasaki
Tanega I.
Kurile Is.
Paramushir I.
Simushir I.
Urup I.
Iturup I.
Kamchatka Pen.
C.Lopatka
Bering Sea
Atka I.
Andreanof Is.
Rat Is.
Near Is.
Komandorskiye Is.
Aleutian Is.
St.Matthew I.
Peking
Wutai Shan
Yellow Sea
Shantung Pen.
Grand Canal
Nanking
Shanghai
Hwang-Ho (Yellow)
Great Plain of China
a Shan
Wuhan
Poyang L.
Wu Yi Shan
Nan Shan
Canton
Hong Kong
St.Kiang
Tung-Ting L.
East China Sea
Amami Is.
Okinawa
Ryu Kyu Is.
Ishigaki I.
Taiwan (Formosa)
Batan Is.
Babuyan Is.
Cheju Do
PACIFIC OCEAN
Bonin Is.
Volcano Is.
G.of Tonking
Hainan
Luzon
Manila
Mindoro
Samar
Panay
Leyte
Negros
Palawan
Mindanao
Sulu Sea
Sulu Arch.
Talaud Is.
Sangit Is.
Celebes Sea
Kinabalu
Balabac Str.
Philippines
Yap Is.
Palau Is.
Caroline Islands
Ca Mau Pt.
Saigon
Cholon
South China Sea
Mekong
Kampuchea
Ataouat
Mui Varella
Borneo
Iran Ra.
Schwaner Ra.
Kapuas
Mahakam
Celebes
Rantemario
Makassar Str.
Halmahera
Waigeo
Molucca Sea
Batjan Is.
Moluccas
Ceram
Buru
Sula Is.
Banda Sea
Kai Is.
Aru Is.
Tanimbar Is.
New Guinea
Biak
Arafura Sea
Bunguran Is.
Greater
Singapore
Riouw Arch.
Lingga Arch.
Bangka
Beliung
Belitung
Java Sea
Djakarta
Semeru
Bali
Sunda Is.
Flores Sea
Flores
Sumba
Sumbawa
Timor
Roti
Alor
Wetar
Butung
Gulf of Tomini

BREAD-FRUIT TREE

RUBBER

CITRUS FRUIT
PEPPER PLANTATION

The biggest freshwater basin in the Eurasian continent (Europe and Asia), Lake Baykal is in southern Siberia, near the city of Irkutsk. The lake has filled an enormous rift valley (produced by subsidence), which is why it is as long as 612 km. Lake Baykal is also the deepest lake in the world—1,741 m. More than 300 streams empty into the lake, but its only outlet is the Angara River, in the south.

At 5,633 m, the highest peak in the Caucasus chain, Mt Elbrus is in the Georgian SSR, in south-western USSR. The Caucasus chain appears unimpressive when seen from the Black Sea, but, farther inland, it suddenly climbs to form a bastion of powerful massifs, deeply marked by erosion. This is where Elbrus is to be found, an ancient volcano, extinct for only a few tens of thousands of years, as indicated by the heavy lava outflows superimposed on the morainic formations, which, in their turn were produced by glacial erosion. More than 20 glaciers descend from the mountain.

AKAN NATIONAL PARK
Japan possesses about 30 national parks, all of modest size, which were formed mainly for scientific purposes and for the spreading of culture. The most interesting is that of Akan, on the island of Hokkaido, which contains, within an area of 875 sq km, vast coniferous forests and as many as five active volcanoes. The sides of the volcanoes are covered in azaleas and rhododendrons, and brown bears and deer live in the forests.

ANATOLIA
The vast Anatolian peninsula (Asia Minor), today completely occupied by Turkey, is one of the most interesting lands of the world for its ancient heritage of history and art, from classical Greece to the beginnings of Christianity. It is also a special region of natural beauty, solemn, mysterious, and remote. The region of Cappadocia, in the east, is a real masterpiece of nature, which has unfortunately been violated by tourism. The huge expanse of volcanic lava and tufa, alternating with mighty layers of basalt, has been intensively attacked by rain, torrents, and wind, creating a 'forest' of pyramids and spires and conical formations known as 'fairy chimneys', sometimes surmounted by precariously perched rocks of harder material.

ANNAPURNA
One of the most extraordinary countries in the world, Nepal lies almost wholly in the Himalaya. It was closed to European travellers until the late 1940s. It consists of a strip of land, 150-240 km wide and 800 km long, on the southern slopes of the Himalaya, commanding all the most important passes between India and China. The first chain of mountains, the Mahabharat Lekh, with peaks over 2,700 m, comes after two parallel belts of hills. Then come the great valleys, after which rises the most beautiful and striking part of the mighty Himalaya mountain range. Several peaks over 7,000 m can be found, and six over 8,000 m, among which are the formidable Annapurna, 8,075 m (the first '8,000' to be climbed in the history of mountaineering, by a French expedition in 1950), and Everest (8,848 m), the 'Roof of the World'.

ARABIAN PENINSULA
Covering an area of about $2\frac{1}{2}$ million sq km, the Arabian Peninsula is mostly deserts (sometimes called collectively the Arabian Desert), which are part of the great system of deserts that stretches from the Sahara to the Gobi Desert without break of continuity. Geographically, the Arabian Peninsula is part of Africa, and the Red Sea can be thought of as part of the huge fracture of the Great Rift Valley. The desert is divided into two areas: the Dahana and Nafud deserts in the north and east and the huge Rub' al Khali ('The Empty Quarter') in the south. In the centre, the heart of Saudi Arabia, is the Najd, a somewhat humid region, covered with fruit trees (date palms, mulberry, pomegranate, peach, fig, and apricot). It is well cultivated (wheat, vines, and barley) and inhabited by domesticated camels (dromedaries).

ASSAM
A state of India, in the extreme north-east, Assam is a special land, unique in certain aspects. Joined to the rest of India by a narrow tortuous corridor, it is bordered on all sides by foreign states: Tibet (China), Bhutan, Burma, and Bangladesh, and is almost enclosed by mountains. It covers over 200,000 sq km and has a population of about 15 million. The Brahmaputra River is a dominant feature of the region. Its broad, fertile valley crosses Assam, bringing with it both wealth and destruction. Whole towns are wiped from the map during the floods, due to the remarkable amount of rain—up to 10,000 mm a year in places. Other disasters are caused by earthquakes. Nevertheless, the climate is pleasant, and the vegetation extremely luxuriant. Assam is sometimes called the 'Land of Orchids', as over 1,000 species grow there. And leopards, tigers, elephants, and rhinoceroses abound in the dense tropical forests.

BARLEY
Barley (*Hordeum vulgare*) belongs to the grass family (Graminae). It was known in prehistoric times, and its edible seeds have been found in lake dwellings. Barley is cultivated over a great area, from Norway to the equator. No other cereal can be grown at greater heights at the same latitude. Barley is

used as animal feed and, as grain (pearled barley), is eaten in soups, or is ground to make bread and baby cereal. Barley is also used, by means of a complicated process, in making beer. The USSR is the world's major producer of barley.

BEARS
The continent of Asia, with its great variety of environments, is the home of various species of bear, belonging to the bear family (Ursidae). The polar bear (*Thalarctos maritimus*), one of the largest living carnivores, lives in the icy polar lands. An expert swimmer, and endowed with an exceptional resistance to cold, it can travel tens of kilometres a day over ice and in the cold waters. The brown bear (*Ursus arctos*) is frequently to be found, particularly in the Himalaya. The Himalayan black bear (*Selenarctos thibetanus*), with the characteristic V-shaped white patch on its chest and neck, lives in central and southern Asia, in China, and in Japan, up to an altitude of 3,000 m. The sloth bear (*Melursus ursinus*), with a black shaggy coat and a white V-shaped patch on its chest, lives in the forests of India and Sri Lanka and the foothills of the Himalaya.

BREAD-FRUIT TREE (see photograph p.23)
A tree of the mulberry (Moraceae) family (*Artocarpus altilis*), it has large, glossy, leathery leaves, divided into lobes with parallel edges, and is found in Malaysia and the Pacific islands. It stands 12-18 m high. It takes its name from the oval or round fruits, 10-20 cm in diameter, with a very starchy pulp, that can be eaten cooked, having a taste similar to potatoes, and looking and feeling like bread. It is a food of special importance in the diet of the native populations.

CAMPHOR TREE
A large tree of the laurel (Lauraceae) family, indigenous to China and Japan, the camphor tree (*Cinnamomum camphora*) is extensively cultivated in tropical regions for camphor, a substance used both in the production of celluloid and cine film and in medicine (as a mild antiseptic and a mouth wash). Camphor is obtained by steam distillation of the wood of the branches. It has a distinctive and penetrating odour. Spirits of camphor, which is used in medicine, is a mixture of camphor, alcohol, and water.

CHOMO LHARI
In the south of Bhutan, along the border with India, lies a region of plains and river valleys, rising to a height of about 1,000 m. The land then rises towards the north, where an impenetrable barrier of peaks and summits is dominated by the solitary Chomo Lhari (Divine Queen of Mountains), 7,314 m high, on the border with Tibet. In the areas below 4,500 m, the landscape is pleasant because of the presence of large forests (ash, oak, poplar, willow) and a rich and varied fauna.

CITRUS FRUIT (see photograph p.23)
This is the name of the various species (and their respective fruits) of the *Citrus* genus of the rue family (Rutaceae). They are small trees requiring a warm climate and almost no frost or wind. Citrus fruits came from southern India, Indochina, and southern China, and, at various periods, became widespread in Europe in those areas with a Mediterranean climate. The species that are cultivated include lemon, orange, mandarin orange (or tangerine), lime, bergamot, citron, grapefruit,

Above: A region of western Asia, situated between the rivers Tigris and Euphrates, Mesopotamia is mainly a land of mountains and extensive desert plateaus. Lowlands, part of the great depression of Mesopotamia, are found only in the south-western corner. The name means 'between the rivers'. Some of the world's earliest civilizations developed in Mesopotamia, which is now mostly part of Iraq.

Right: Situated in south-western Turkey, Pamukkale is a wonder of nature. Hot springs, laden with minerals, deposit several tonnes of limestone a year, producing cataracts of chalk-white cliffs. Pamukkale is Turkish for 'cotton fortress'.

Mount Ararat is the beautiful mountain where Noah's ark is supposed to have lodged. It rises in eastern Turkey, near the border with Iran and the USSR, and is the cone of an extinct volcano which today is covered largely in ice. Ice overflowing from the craters down the sides of the volcano, like huge, suddenly halted lava outflows, makes a superb spectacle. At 5,165 m, Ararat is the highest mountain in Turkey.

The Gobi, a cold, treeless desert in central Asia, extends from Mongolia and Manchuria to eastern Turkestan. It is a plateau, 900-1,200 m high, consisting of vast expanses of windswept sands and rock and gravel, marshy in places and swept by violent storms. Because of the very dry climate, it is poor in flora and fauna. In very ancient times, the area was probably a sea, which later dried up; remains of dinosaurs have been found there. Now, in some areas, only the occasional camel, surviving in the wild, can be found.

A herbaceous plant *(Cannabis sativa)* of the Cannabinaceae family, hemp is indigenous to central and western Asia, and widely cultivated in both tropical and temperate regions. The fibres, used in the manufacture of rope, string, and strong cloth, are obtained from the stems, which are first soaked and then submitted to various mechanical processes. An oil is obtained from the seeds which is used for soaps and paints. The seeds themselves are used for bird-feed. A resin obtained from the leaves and other tissues is a source of marijuana (cannabis).

and kumquat. Citrus fruits, rich in vitamins (particularly C), are eaten fresh or used in sweetmeats, candied fruits, etc. The essences obtained from the peel are used in perfumes, liqueurs, syrups, and medicines.

DEAD SEA
The lowest body of water on the Earth's surface, the Dead Sea is famous both for its Biblical tradition and for its physical characteristics. It is called by various names in the Bible, and that of the Dead Sea occurs only once. The Romans called it the 'asphalt lake'. The Dead Sea stretches for 74 km from north to south. It has a maximum width of 16 km and an area of 960 sq km. Its surface is 395 m below sea level, and it has a maximum depth of 400 m. The River Jordan keeps it well supplied with water, but evaporation is very rapid. The nauseating, foetid waters have a salinity content seven times greater than that of the oceans. The waters are so dense that a person can float on the surface without any effort.

EBONY
A heavy, hard, and compact wood, obtainable from various trees of the *Diospyros* genus of the ebony family (Ebenaceae), ebony is wide-

spread throughout India, Sri Lanka, south-east Asia, and the Far East. It can be reddish, yellow, white, or brownish in colour, but the typical colour is black. It has such a fine grain that it can be polished like a mirror. It is brittle, but is easy to work and carve. It is used in wood inlays of furniture, handles, black piano keys, and ornamental objects.

ELBURZ MOUNTAINS
On the Caspian Sea, the coast of Iran is edged by a chain of extraordinary mountains, the Elburz range, a majestic, desert barrier. They rise up as sheer walls from the Caspian depression, with rocky sides weathered by the wind, which has scored millions and millions of little niches into them. In the more inland areas, the chain has been incised by arid and desolate valleys, along the bottom of which can be found oases, where the aquifer (permeable rock holding water) is close to the surface. The chain is dominated, near Tehran, by the permanently snow-covered peak of Demavend, an extinct volcanic cone that rises to 5,771 m.

EQUATORIAL FOREST
In equatorial regions with a very hot, humid climate and heavy rainfall, a dense, evergreen forest dominates the landscape. This type of forest is divided into layers: an undergrowth, rich in ferns and grasses; a shrub layer; a layer of middle-sized plants; a layer including the majority of tall plants which, with their foliage, form the 'dome' of the forest; and, finally, the foliage of the tallest trees, emerging over the dome. Parasitic plants live at the expense of others, clinging tightly to the host plant. Epiphyte plants prosper on more sturdy plants, in search of air and sun. Various climbing plants, and many huge lianas, wrap themselves around the trunks and stems, forming an impenetrable tangle. The sun almost never reaches the floor of the equatorial forest.

FUR ANIMALS
In the cold regions of the world there are many species of animals with valuable fur. In the USSR (as in Scandinavia and North America), fur animals are hunted by organized companies, which sell the skins on the great fur markets (London, New York, Leipzig, and Leningrad). Farms have been created in these regions for breeding those fur animals that adapt more easily to life in

Right: Cedars are a group of majestic conifers of the pine (Pinaceae) family, with plentiful foliage and a strong trunk. They live a very long time, and various species are widespread throughout Asia Minor, central Asia, and north Africa. The cedar of Lebanon *(Cedrus libani),* which was already famous in ancient times (its wood being used for shipbuilding by the Phoenicians, Egyptians, Assyrians, and Babylonians), is found, not only in the Lebanon, but also in the neighbouring mountain chains, where it forms extensive woods. The deodar *(Cedrus deodara)* is found throughout the Himalaya at a height of between 1,000 and 2,300 m. The Atlas cedar *(Cedrus atlantica)* belongs to the Atlas chain, in Algeria and Morocco. Cedars are grown as ornamental plants for parks and gardens.

captivity, such as the mink and the blue fox. The animals that supply the most valuable furs are the mink, ermine, sable, marten, fox, otter, and beaver.

HIMALAYA
The highest mountain range in the world, the Himalaya form an arc, 2,500 km long and as much as 300 km wide, across southern Asia. They lie in the north of the Indian subcontinent, bordered by Pakistan, India, and China and completely enclosing Nepal and Bhutan. This titanic bastion, called 'the land of snows', includes more than 100 peaks over 6,000 m, 33 over 7,200 m, and 14 over 8,000 m. Everest, at 8,848 m, is the highest mountain in the world. The Himalaya have an alpine climate and abundant rain on the Indian side (as much as 2,500 mm annually). Tropical plants such as the palm and fig grow on the southern slopes, up to a height of 1,000 m, and oak and chestnut trees are found up to 2,000 m. Tea is cultivated up to 1,500 m and rice and corn up to nearly 2,000 m.

The yak *(Bos grunniens)* is a huge ox, living in a semi-domesticated state in the mountainous areas of central Asia (particularly in Tibet), between altitudes of 4,000 and 6,000 m. The yak resembles the bison, with its widely separated horns, the hump over its withers, and the long, thick fur over its hindquarters that sweeps the ground like a fringe. It is an agile climber and a strong swimmer. It defies gales and blizzards by crowding together with its companions. It can survive at −40° C. If there is nothing else to feed on, it will eat mosses and lichens, quenching its thirst with snow.

JUTE
A vegetable textile fibre, third in economic and practical importance after cotton and hemp, jute is supplied by various species of *Corchorus,* a genus of very tall, perennial grasses of the basswood (Tiliaceae) family, indigenous to India, where it is also extensively cultivated. Jute fibre is obtained from stalks left to soak in water for about 10 days. The fibres are stripped from the stalks in strands of 2-3 m, washed, and dried in the sun. Jute is used for weaving coarse cloth, sacks, tarpaulins, and ropes.

KAMCHATKA PENINSULA
In the east, Siberia terminates in the 'appendix' of the Kamchatka Peninsula, which covers an area of 270,000 sq km. It is a product of the Pliocene Era, when a huge uplift movement reactivated the rivers and volcanoes. Today, the peninsula can be seen as a greatly eroded plain from which rise some 60 volcanoes, 10 of them active. The highest of these is Klyuchevskaya Sopka (4,750 m), which lights up the polar nights with its eruptions and the rumbling of which can be heard 250 km away. The Kamchatka Peninsula continues south into the Kuril Islands. These 32 islands have active volcanoes, the lower slopes of which are covered with beautiful forests.

KARAKORAM
West of Tibet, the Himalaya range continues naturally into the Karakoram range, which encloses the region of Kashmir. The name means 'black gravel'. The southern face of the Karakoram is lapped by the majestic course of the Indus. The second-highest peak in the world, Godwin Austin (K2), rises from the chain, 8,611 m high. It was first conquered by an Italian expedition in 1954. The Karakoram Pass, 5,575 m above sea level, is the highest in the world, and is the chief route between Kashmir and China.

KARA KUM
Literally 'the Black desert', the Kara Kum has an area of about 300,000 sq km, and occupies most of Turkmenistan, a republic of the USSR. Sandy and undulating, the desert provides all-year pasturage for sheep and goats. The north is an area of shallow waves of sand. The south consists of dunes interspersed with *takyrs,* platforms of salt flats. The land is irrigated by the 800-km Kara Kum Canal, completed in 1962.

KINABALU
At 4,101 m above sea level, Mount Kinabalu is the highest peak on the island of Borneo. An isolated granite peak, it lies in Sabah, near the northern tip of the island. The mountain is a superb sight, standing clearly outlined in the sun, often over a thick bank of clouds. A national park has been formed around it, containing all species of tropical flora, from that of the equatorial forest to the rare and scrubby flora of the bare rocks above 3,500 m. The orang-utan lives there at liberty.

LEMMINGS
Lemmings (genus *Lemmus*) are small rodents of the same family (Cricetidae) as, and similar to, hamsters and voles. They live in the cold regions of Europe, Asia, and North America. They are prolific, voracious, and aggressive, live in crowded colonies, and tunnel underground. Periodically, because of an increase in their capacity to reproduce (increasing from 2 annual births of 5 young to 4 annual births of 6-8 young), there is, in some years, an exceptional increase in their number. In consequence, lemmings set off on great migrations, not even stopping before rivers and lakes, across which they swim at the cost of serious decimation. These particular migrations, which commence in autumn, end in winter with the almost total destruction of the migrant hordes.

LENA RIVER
This is the longest river in Siberia and one of the longest rivers in the world, flowing for 4,800 km. It is a typical plateau river, receiving the contributions of large tributaries, which are erosively very active and bring down with them great masses of detritus, including alluvium that is rich in platinum and gold. The water is very low in winter, when the river freezes. The delta on the Arctic Ocean (about 400 km wide) is the last to melt, and this, together with the heavy summer rains, brings disastrous floods.

MALAY ARCHIPELAGO
In the south-east, the continent of Asia breaks up into an immense archipelago—the biggest in the world—of about 10,000 islands. The total surface area of these islands is about 2½ million sq km. They lie between south-eastern Asia and Australia, and include the Lesser Sunda Islands, New Guinea, the Moluccas, and the Philippines. This world of land and

Bamboo is the name of various species of the grass (Gramineae) family, which make up the subfamily Bambusoideae. They are widespread throughout the hot regions of the world, and typical of southern and eastern Asia. Some species of bamboo reach a height of over 30 m. The hollow, woody stems are divided into segments and are very light, but strong. They are used as fishing poles and in housing, handicrafts, tools, papermaking, etc. Some species of bamboo flower irregularly at intervals, even decades apart.

Tea (Camellia sinensis) is a plant of the Theaceae family, indigenous to China. It is widely cultivated in tropical areas for its leaves, from which the beverage tea is obtained. Depending on the method of preparation, there is green tea, the leaves of which are dried after harvesting, and black tea, the leaves of which have also been allowed to ferment. In the wild, the tea plant grows as high as 10 m, but on plantations it is a small, branching shrub, kept to 1-2 m by pruning. Tea is the habitual drink of the peoples of the Far East. The practice of tea-drinking was introduced into Europe in the 1600s. The main tea producers are India, Sri Lanka, China, and Japan.

Left: Orang-utans. These huge anthropoid apes (Pongo pygmaeus), which the Malays call 'men of the woods' (orang=man; utan=woods), because of their resemblance to man, live in the humid forests of Sumatra and Borneo. Mild-tempered, despite their huge size (they can reach a height of 1.5 m and a weight of 100 kg), the orangs live in trees alone or in small groups, deep in the forests, feeding mainly on fruit. They rarely come down from the trees. They are endowed with exceptional strength and have practically no enemies. The natives of Borneo claim that orangs can successfully tackle even crocodiles, and are capable of biting a python to death.

The Mekong River rises in eastern Tibet and flows south through Indochina for about 4,200 km before it empties into the South China Sea through several mouths. Just below Phnom Penh, the capital of the Khmer Republic, the river splits into three branches: two enter Vietnam and the third remains in the Khmer Republic, forming Lake Tonle Sap. Here a phenomenon occurs which is unique in the world: from July to October, during the rainy season, the waters flow from the Mekong to the lake; from November to June, they return from the lake to the Mekong.

sea, which straddles the equator, was formed about 2 million years ago, as the great ice-sheets retreated. The rise in sea level, though only 30 m, caused this chain of islands to be cut off from the continent, as evidenced by the shallow continental shelves between the main islands and the continent.

MALAY PENINSULA

Relatively recent geological movements have detached the Malay Peninsula from the Malay Archipelago. The nearness of the equator and the sea makes the mainly volcanic Malay Peninsula a treasure-house of mineral wealth and a natural paradise of luxuriant and swampy forests. There are several wildlife reserves, the largest being the Taman Negara National Park, created around Gunong Tahan, the highest peak in the Malay Peninsula (2,190 m), on the boundary of Pahang and Kelantan. It includes elephant, deer (muntjac and sambar), the Malayan tapir, and the Sumatran rhinoceros.

NEGEV DESERT

This is not only a marvel of nature, but even more a marvel of man's labours. The desert occupies the whole of the southern part of the state of Israel and is divided into three distinct zones. In the south are the mountains of Eilat, crystalline rocks with a maximum height of 900 m and almost entirely arid. In the centre are mountains, forming three parallel chains, about 1,000 m high, heavily eroded and scarred by deep canyons along which rush short-lived torrents, lined with sparse vegetation. In the north, there are hills and gentle slopes to which Israel has brought water, creating orchards and fields of crops. The water is pumped from the Sea of Galilee through a 140-km system of canals, pipelines, and tunnels, and then through a network that extends to the southern Negev.

OB RIVER

Of the great Siberian rivers, the Ob is distinguished, not only by its length (4,000 km) and its enormous basin (some 3 million sq km), but also for a few curious characteristics. In autumn, after the great floods, its waters assume a reddish colour and become repugnant and fatal to fish. In addition, the mouth of the river becomes remarkably dilated, and the drowned lower course forms a huge gulf, 80 km wide and no less than 800 km long, in the Arctic Ocean.

PAMIR KNOT

This is a high-altitude region of central Asia, meeting place of great mountain chains: the Himalaya (Karakoram), Hindu Kush, Tien Shan, and Kunlun. Pamir, or the Pamirs, called by the natives Bam-i-Dunya, 'roof of the world', is one of the highest plateaus in the world, a lifeless desert of rugged mountains cut by deep canyons, with steppes and salt lakes at intervals. It lies mainly in the USSR (Tadzhikstan), but also on the borders of China (Sinkiang), Kashmir, and Afghanistan. Its highest peak, in the Muztagh Ata range, is Kungur (7,665 m), in China. Also in the Pamir Knot is Russia's highest mountain, Communism Peak (7,495 m).

PANDAS

This is the name of two carnivorous mammals that are not related. The giant panda (Ailuropoda melanoleuca), discovered last century in the mountains of China, was first attributed to the bear (Ursidae) family, but it is more closely related to the racoon (Procyonidae) family, to which it really belongs by character and constitution. It resembles a young bear, and has characteristic black and white fur. It lives in the bamboo forests in the mountains of south-western China, and feeds almost entirely on the shoots of these plants, but is also known to eat birds and small mammals. Because of its rarity and its attractive appearance, it has been adopted as the symbol of the World Wildlife Fund, the international organization that exists for the conservation of wildlife and of animal and vegetable species in danger of extinction. The lesser panda *(Ailurus fulgens)* is the size of a large cat, has a thick, bright red fur, and lives in the Himalaya forests. Also called the red, or common, panda, it is usually placed in a special family, the Ailuridae, closely related to the racoons.

PHEASANTS
Some of the most beautiful species of birds, pheasants belong to the Phasianidae family, which is widespread throughout the Asian continent. Among the most renowned for their elegant and multicoloured plumage are the true pheasant *(Phasianus colchicus)*, often a guest in zoological gardens; the golden pheasant, with its splendid purple and gold livery, and the silver, or argus, pheasant. But the member of the family that surpasses them all for elegance of shape and splendour of costume is the peacock *(Pavo cristatus)*, indigenous to southern India and mentioned in the Bible as one of the most valuable and sought-after creatures of ancient times. Greatly appreciated by the Romans and in the Middle Ages for its exquisite flesh, it is bred today as an 'ornament' for parks and gardens.

RUBBER (see photograph p.23)
Natural rubber is obtained from many species of plant, the most important being *Hevea brasiliensis*, a tree of the Euphorbiaceae family, indigenous to Brazil, and it was well known, even in the pre-Columbus era. Today, as well as in its country of origin, it is cultivated in Sri Lanka, Malaysia, Indonesia, and Indochina. The valuable latex flows from incisions made in the trunk and is collected in cups. Crude rubber is obtained by straining the latex and coagulating it with formic acid. The practical and economic importance of natural rubber has greatly diminished with the invention and use of synthetic rubber.

RUHUNU NATIONAL PARK
This is the most famous of Sri Lanka's national parks, the one that best represents the features of this beautiful island. It extends from the sands of Sri Lanka's south-east coast, across plains and lagoons, to the forest. The greater part of its 620 sq km is covered by brushwood, with tall trees along the river banks. The visitor is fascinated by the extraordinary fauna: the bears prefer the grassy plains, the elephants require certain types of tree because of the leaves, crocodiles live in the rivers, and the Komodo dragon, the largest living lizard (2-3 m long), is seen on the rocks. Some 200 species of birds live in the trees of the park.

SCREW PINE
Shrubs or trees of the *Pandanus* genus of the Pandanaceae family, screw pines grow in the Malay Archipelago and the tropical regions of Asia, Africa, and Australia. Some species are cultivated for the fibres that can be obtained from the long, narrow, leathery leaves, and from which mats, baskets, and ropes are made. Other species are grown for their edible fruits, yet others as ornamental plants.

The most southerly of China's three great rivers, the Si-Kiang (West River) is 2,000 km long. It is known in its upper (western) course as the Hungshui. In the eastern part of its course it crosses a landscape of marvellous scenery; formed by mountains shaped like cones or towers, the result of the decomposition of a karst region extending over thousands of years. This scenery is a recurrent theme in classical Chinese painting.

SINAI PENINSULA
Bounded by the Gulf of Suez on the west and the Gulf of Aqaba on the east, the Sinai Peninsula juts into the Red Sea. It is regarded by most geographers as part of Asia, although it is politically controversial, having been occupied by Israel in 1967. It partially reproduces, in miniature, the Arabian Desert: the south is delineated by a crystalline massif, culminating in the Gebel Katherina, 2,637 m high and well endowed with oases; and to the north extend various limestone plateaus, deserts of sand and rock that are totally uninhabited. Towards the Mediterranean, Sinai ends in a series of salty lagoons and sandy dunes, completely hostile to human settlement. The Biblical Mount Sinai is thought to be one of the peaks on the peninsula, but scholars cannot agree which one it is.

SPICES
Spices are obtained from certain vegetable parts (seeds, fruits, bark, buds, peel, etc.) that contain flavours, and are, therefore, used as seasoning or in the preparation of medicines, cosmetics, and perfumes. Many plants from hot countries were known even in ancient times for the spices they provided, spices so rare and sought after that they were imported from the Orient and sold in the West at very high prices. Their countries of origin were unknown until, first the Portuguese, then the Dutch, organized expeditions to discover them. Having once found them, they retained for a long time a spice monopoly, making huge profits. Although, nowadays, spices have become simple accessories in cooking, once, when there was no other way to keep meat for a long time, their use was indispensable both for the actual preservation of food and for concealing unpleasant smells and tastes. The most popular spices include:
Cinnamon, made from the bark of *Cinnamomum zeylanicum,* a tree of the laurel (Lauraceae) family, cultivated on the island of Sri Lanka. The bark of the young branches is peeled off in long strips, and curls into rolls on drying. It is used in cooking and to flavour liqueurs, pastries, and other foodstuffs.
Clove, from the flower buds of *Eugenia caryophyllata,* a small tree of the Myrtaceae family, indigenous to the Moluccas. Gathered when immature and then dried, the buds are used to flavour food and drink.
Nutmeg, the woody and aromatic seed, or

Teak is a hard, tough wood, dark red in colour, produced by the *Tectona grandis*, a tall tree of the Verbenaceae family, indigenous to India and south-eastern Asia. It is extremely durable and strong, and is used in industrial construction and shipbuilding. It is also used for furniture, being easily worked, of moderate weight, and able to take a high polish. The tree reaches heights of up to 45 m.

Left: The Ganges, sacred river of India and the Hindu religion. Rising in the Himalaya and flowing through very narrow valleys, it is 2,500 km long, and empties into the Bay of Bengal through a vast delta, some 300 km across. At the delta, 400 km from the sea, it receives the waters of the Brahmaputra. Millions of Hindus constantly crowd the banks of the Ganges, to bathe in the water, particularly in the holy cities of Benares and Allahabad. Some go to purify themselves or cure their ailments. And to die on its banks and give one's ashes to the waters of the river is considered to be the way to Paradise.

kernel, of *Myristica fragrans,* a tree of the nutmeg (Myrtaceae) family, indigenous to the Moluccas. It is the source of two spices for flavouring food—whole or ground nutmeg from the inner seed, and mace from the seed covering that separates it from the husk. Also extracted from the nutmeg are butters and an oil used in medicines and toilet preparations.

Pepper, the fruit of plants of the pepper (Piperaceae) family, indigenous to Indonesia. Black pepper is obtained from the fruits of *Piper nigrum,* which are gathered when unripe and dried; white pepper, less 'hot', comes from the fruit of the same plant, gathered ripe and peeled after soaking. Pepper is used as a seasoning and to flavour salted meat (see photograph p.23).

SUNDA VOLCANOES

The islands and islets of Indonesia, in the Sunda Archipelago, are often violently shaken by the sudden eruption of the still-active volcanoes. The worst eruption was that of Krakatoa, a volcanic island in the Sunda Strait, between Sumatra and Java. The volcano erupted in 1883, and the neighbouring islands were hit by gigantic tidal waves which claimed 35,000 victims. Volcanic ash continued to fall for over a year. In 1963, Mount Agung on the island of Bali erupted three times, claiming 1,500 lives and a third of Bali's farmland, leaving 85,000 people homeless.

TIBET

An independent country before the Chinese invasion in the early 1950s, Tibet is the highest and most extensive area of China, an 'ocean' of nearly impenetrable mountains, enclosing almost unknown and inaccessible basins. Often called 'the roof of the world', its features vary from grandiose folding phenomena to rocky plateaus; from morainic hills to alluvial plains; from gigantic alluvial cones to volcanoes. It is roughly divided into two parts. Northern Tibet is an enclosed plateau between 4,000 and 6,000 m high, containing hundreds of fresh- and salt-water lakes. Southern Tibet is a great depression reaching towards the Himalayas and the slopes of Mt Everest in the south. The cradle of Buddhism, Tibet is a land of great monasteries. Lhasa, the ancient capital, is the 'land of the gods', in which may be found the Potala, the ancient residence of the Dalai Lama, the spiritual leader of the Tibetans.

TUNDRA

The tundra, a vast area with perpetually frozen subsoil, stretches along the shores of the Arctic Ocean from Scandinavia to the Kamchatka Peninsula, the eastern tip of Siberia. The name comes from the Finnish 'Tunturi', and means a marshy plain. The tundra begins where coniferous forests end, and stretches northwards as far as the border of eternal

Near Kyoto, in Japan, the beautiful wooded Jakkoin Garden is the carefully thought-out result of long labour, extending through the centuries, to combine colours, optical effects, and serene and moving scenery in every season. The garden was begun in the 1100s by a Japanese empress, who built her own tomb there.

snows and ice. In winter, the temperature drops as low as −50° C; in summer, the surface ice melts, and mosses and lichens appear, along with some flowering plants. The tundra is the kingdom of the reindeer and caribou.

WALRUS

Walruses make up the Odòbenidae family of the seals (order, Pinnipedia). They are huge animals, some 3.5 m long and weighing up to 1,350 kg. They are characterized by a body perfectly adapted to water life, and by two enormous protruding upper canine teeth, developed (in the males) like tusks. In spite of being hunted for its skin, blubber, and ivory, the walrus is still quite numerous today. The animals live in huge herds on the coast and on ice floes in the extreme north of Asia, Europe, and North America. The Pacific walrus *(Odobenus divergens)* is found in the Bering Sea, and has tusks as long as 75-100 cm.

WILD HORSES

In the region of desert and steppe between Siberia and western China, the last wild horses can still be found. They are called Przhevalski's horses or tarpans *(Equus przewalskii),* short and thickset in shape. They are smaller than most domestic horses, standing about 135 cm at the shoulders, with a greyish-brown coat and brown mane and tail. They live in herds of about 15 animals, led by an old stallion. Proud and wild-tempered, they defend their freedom by kicking and biting. If captured young, they adapt to life in captivity, but still keep their tempestuous character.

YANGTZE KIANG

The fourth longest river in the world, and the longest and most important in China. The Chinese simply call it *Kiang,* 'the river'. It rises in the Kunlun Mountains of Tibet, 4,800 m above sea level, and flows 5,500 km into the East China Sea, near Shanghai. Half of the Chinese population lives in its basin, which has an area of nearly 2 million sq km. The delta is an extensive and very fertile region, criss-crossed by a maze of canals, the most complicated in the world.

YENISEY RIVER

One of the longest rivers in the USSR, the Yenisey is about 4,500 km long. Its name means 'the great water'. Near its source, there are very swift rapids. Farther on, it receives the immense contribution of the Angara, the main effluent of Lake Baykal, and then slowly flows through the tundra, where it is 3-4 km wide, and into the Arctic Ocean, where it has a wide estuary. The most significant features of the Yenisey are its banks. The right bank is high and rocky, and covered in forests; the left bank is low and covered in grassland, where the great Siberian plain ends.

YUNNAN

The Chinese province of Yunnan, in the south of the country, is geologically one of the most interesting on the continent. Folding movements of the Earth's crust have produced great tabular formations that have been eroded, over thousands of years, both by surface elements and by underground water. A labyrinth of caves was first formed, the subsidence of which produced sink-holes and funnel-shaped depressions, comprising an extraordinary display of limestone transformed into spires and pinnacles—hence the name 'the stone forest'.

Above: The sacred mountain of Japan, Mt Fuji is a beautiful, almost perfectly conical extinct volcano, 3,776 m high, the distinctive shape of which has become a symbol of the country to the rest of the world. On the summit, crowned with eternal snows, is the crater, 600 m wide. It last erupted in 1707. Its real name is Fuji-san, but as a result of a past error the name Fujiyama has stuck. At all seasons of the year, the majestic and graceful cone of the volcano has an indescribable fascination that only Japanese poetry and paintings have been able to portray.

Right: Mount Taal. Situated in the south of the island of Luzon, in the Philippines, Lake Taal has a feature that is unique: at its centre is the island of Volcano, 22 km in circumference; and on Volcano Island stands the 300-metre-high Mt Taal, which has had a number of recorded eruptions since the 1700s. And its cone itself contains a small lake.

Along the tropical sea coasts, in the brackish lagoons exposed to the ebb and flow of the tide, are wide belts of vegetation of the type called 'mangrove'. This kind of vegetation is formed by trees belonging, mainly, to the Rizophoraceae family. Mangrove trees are particularly adapted to a lagoon evironment: they have supporting roots like stilts, or buttresses, descending from the branches and sinking into the ground, and breathing roots (pneumatophores) which rise vertically from the mud and water to carry oxygen to the submerged parts. The seeds often germinate and produce a seedling while the fruit is still attached to the branch; the already well-developed little plant then falls to the mud, puts down roots, and develops into a new tree.

31

AFRICA

With an area of 30 million sq km, Africa is the second largest continent in the world. Some of its features are unique: the most dramatic is the Great Rift Valley, the enormous fissure that stretches down almost the whole length of eastern Africa; and the Sahara, in northern Africa, is the largest desert in the world. Other major features include the Nile, the world's longest river; the Zaïre basin, exceeded in area only by that of the Amazon; Lake Victoria, the second largest in the world; and Lake Tanganyika, the longest and the second deepest. And Africa's highest mountain, Kilimanjaro (5,888 m), although it stands near the equator, is topped with a covering of ice and snow all the year round.

More significant than these bare statistics are Africa's climates, most of which have two characteristics in common—sustained heat and marked seasonality of rainfall. The rain, however, is unevenly spread. Even in the rainiest regions, the differences in the amount of rain falling between two consecutive days, months, or seasons may be enormous. This governs the responses of plants and animals. It divides the year into times of plant activity and dormancy. It also encourages a great diversity of vegetation, which can be divided roughly into an alpine area, consisting of the high mountains of eastern Africa with an infinite variety of rare and strange plants, and a southern subtropical area, with well over 25,000 species of plants. In between the two extends the tropical forest, luxuriant and impenetrable. From forest to desert, on the ground, in the rivers, and in the skies, lives a fantastically rich world of animals, the richest on Earth.

The African elephant *(Loxodonta africana)* is the largest of all land animals, standing as much as 3.5 m at the shoulders and weighing 5-6 tonnes. It lives in central southern Africa, in the forest areas rich in lakes and rivers. Indiscriminately hunted in the past for its ivory tusks, it is now assured of survival in parks and reserves, where hunting is controlled or forbidden. The African elephant lives in herds, and is a creature of habit, always following the same routes. If one is wounded, its companions will always attempt to rescue it. In the picture can be seen an adult elephant, outlined against the majestic background of Kilimanjaro.

Left: Cape Point, in South Africa, is the extreme southern point on the Cape of Good Hope peninsula. A panoramic road climbs to a splendid observation point of tabular rocks, covered with bushes and trees bearing beautiful blossoms. There is a striking contrast between the peaceful vegetation and the ocean thrashing against the wild rocks.

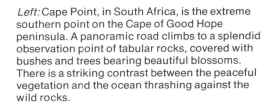

Above: Tassili N'Ajjer is a rocky plateau of the Sahara, in eastern Algeria. It has two distinct features: one is a sandstone plateau, marked by erosion (hamada region); the other is a sand and pebble desert from which rise eroded towers of fantastic shapes and colours, with a sharply serrated outline—the result of water courses (long disappeared) and of the wind.

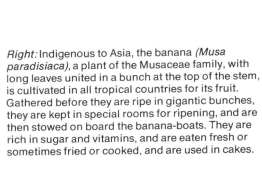

Left: The High Atlas is a range of mountains stretching across central Morocco, from the Atlantic to its eastern border, some 780 km. Most of the peaks are over 2,000 m, rising to 4,165 m at Jebel Toubkal, south of Marrakech. Many of the slopes are covered with forests, enclosing fertile cultivated valleys. The typical tree from 2,000 to 2,750 m is the Atlas cedar *(Cedrus atlantica).* Alpine meadows are found up to 3,200 m. The evergreen oak is the most important tree of the western chains, the red juniper *(Juniperus phoenicea)* of the east. To the south, rivers run through wild gorges and desolate rocks to the Sahara.

Right: Indigenous to Asia, the banana *(Musa paradisiaca),* a plant of the Musaceae family, with long leaves united in a bunch at the top of the stem, is cultivated in all tropical countries for its fruit. Gathered before they are ripe in gigantic bunches, they are kept in special rooms for ripening, and are then stowed on board the banana-boats. They are rich in sugar and vitamins, and are eaten fresh or sometimes fried or cooked, and are used in cakes.

AFRICA - PHYSICAL

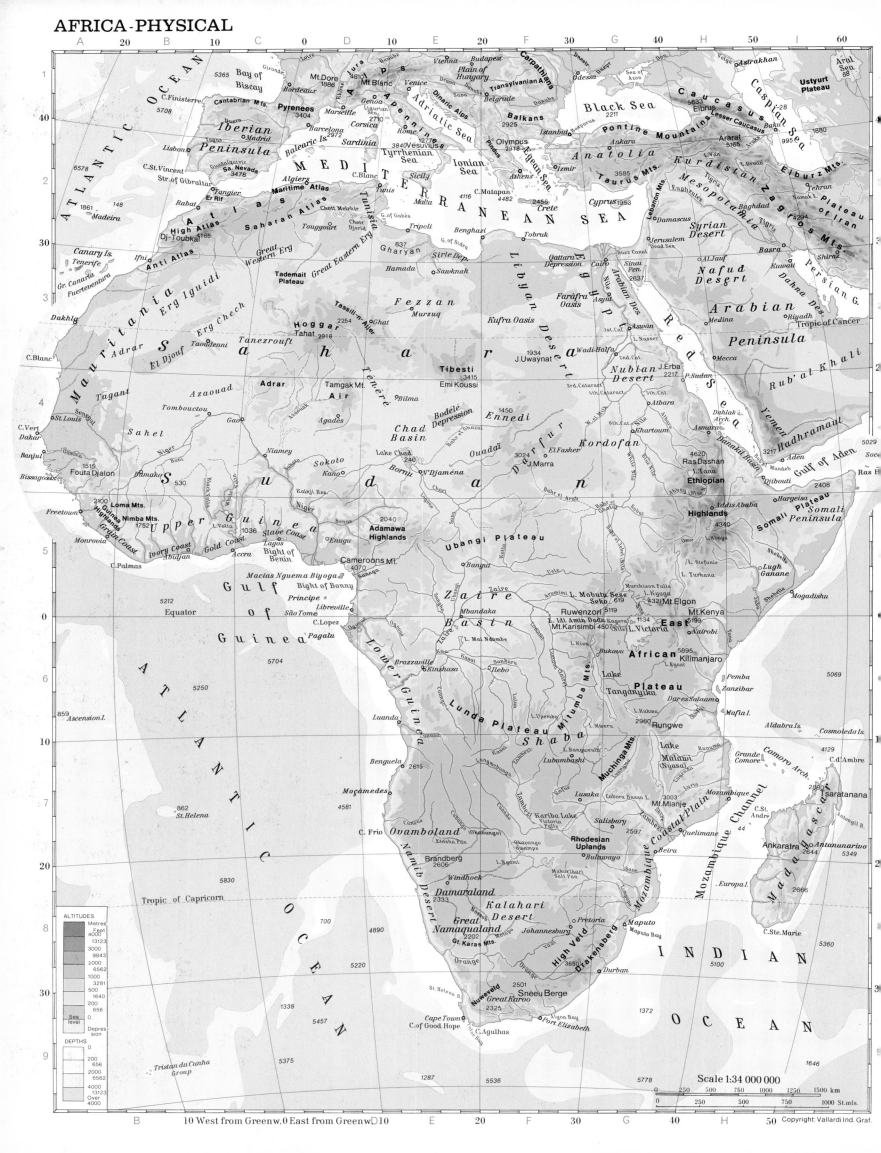

ACACIAS

Acacias (Leguminosae family) are very common on the savannas and steppes of central Africa, and they are a characteristic feature of the scenery of those regions. They are trees or shrubs with bipinnate leaves and spikes of flowers or short-stemmed single blooms. They may bear thorns of various sizes at the base of the leaves (those of some species are 10 cm long). Some African species, such as *Acacia senegal* and *A. arabica*, produce gum arabic, which they secrete spontaneously or after incisions have been made in the bark. Gum arabic is sometimes called 'gum acacia'. It is used in adhesives, inks, polishes, textile finishing, and medicines.

ALOE (see photograph right)

This is a thick-leafed plant of the lily (Liliaceae) family, including some 200 species, mostly South African. They are bushes or small trees (in a few cases quite large trees), with fleshy or thorny leaves. The flowers are united on spikes or in bunches, while the fruits are capsules and bear many seeds. Some species contain resins which, in small doses, are a tonic and aid digestion, while in large doses they are highly laxative. Many species are cultivated as ornamental plants in the open air in Mediterranean regions, or in flower-pots in collections of cactus plants and succulents.

CAPE BUFFALO

The Cape buffalo (*Syncerus caffer*) is the largest bovid in Africa, with a proud, majestic bearing, a sturdy body, sparse black hair, and large, curved out-turned horns, which are very thick at the base. In the last century it was widespread throughout central southern Africa in herds of thousands, but towards the end of the century the Cape buffalo were decimated by a terrible epidemic of cattle plague. Today they are again quite numerous in various areas near lakes and rivers. They are irascible and ferocious, and when attacked they charge with heads held high and at great speed. They are very dangerous to hunt and are feared by hunters more than the lion. Unlike the Indian buffalo, the Cape buffalo has never been domesticated.

CHIMPANZEE

An anthropoid ape, the chimpanzee (*Pan troglodytes*) is the most intelligent of apes and the one that is closest to man in its anatomical and physiological features. It lives in the African equatorial forest in large troops of up to 50 animals, formed by several families consisting of one old male, a few females, and many young ones. By day, the chimpanzees wander about the forest, looking for their food—fruit, leaves, insects, etc. At dusk, they build platforms in the trees, where they spend the night. Because of their intelligence and a good memory, they adapt well to life in captivity and can be trained (especially the young ones) to play games and do exercises of some difficulty.

DRAGON TREE (see photograph right)

The dragon tree is a plant of the lily (Liliaceae) family, resembling the palm, widespread throughout tropical and southern Africa, as well as Arabia and Malaysia. It is a tree or shrub, and the flowers grow in panicles. A reddish resin called 'dragon's blood' is secreted from cracks in the trunk of some species, such as *Dracaena draco* of the Canary Islands, and this resin is used for the production of varnishes. Some species are cultivated as ornamental plants.

GIRAFFE

The giraffe (*Giraffa camelopardalis*) is the tallest of living creatures, with a height, from the horns to the front hooves, of as much as 6 m. The neck, which may be 2 m long, has only 7 cervical vertebrae (neckbones), which is the same as man and mouse have. Found throughout central Africa, the giraffe lives in the sparse undergrowth (protected in parks and reserves), preferably feeding on acacia leaves.

GORILLA

An anthropoid ape, the gorilla (*Gorilla gorilla*) is the largest of the apes, some reaching a height of 2 m and a weight of 250 kg. Despite its imposing appearance and exceptional strength, the gorilla is mild-tempered and peace-loving. It lives in family groups of up to 30 animals, led by an old male. The gorilla inhabits the forests of western central Africa, up to an altitude of as much as 4,000 m in the mountains. It spends the day looking for food, mainly vegetable, on the ground. At night it sleeps in family groups on solid platforms, on the ground or in trees.

GREAT RIFT VALLEY

This is one of the most marked natural phenomena on Earth. It is a huge crack in the Earth's crust, stretching from the valley of the Jordan, in Syria, through the Dead Sea and the Gulf of Aqaba, along the Red Sea, and continuing, through the great Ethiopian depression, into Kenya, Tanzania, and Malawi, as far as Mozambique, including all the great African lakes. A west branch of the Rift Valley extends from the northern end of Lake Malawi and includes lakes Tanganyika, Kivu, Edward, and Albert. Lake Victoria lies on a plateau between the two branches. In the vicinity of the Rift Valley are Mt Kenya and Mt Kilimanjaro, examples of volcanic activity. The complex system of depressions that make up the Great Rift Valley result from ancient movements of the Earth's crust. The altitude of the Great Rift Valley varies from below sea level at the Dead Sea to over 1,800 m above sea level in southern Kenya.

HIPPOPOTAMUS

The hippopotamus (*Hippopotamus amphibius*) is, except for the elephant and the rhinoceros, the largest land mammal on Earth. Found throughout equatorial Africa, near the rivers, lakes, and swamps, the hippopotamus lives in herds of 20-30 animals. It spends most of the day in the water, where it is an agile swimmer and can stay submerged for several minutes. When it re-emerges to breathe, only it eyes, nostrils, and ears protrude from the surface of the water. At sunset, the hippopotamus moves onto the land in search of thick grass, shoots, and leaves. Although of a mild and tranquil nature, it is sometimes seized by panic, which makes it very dangerous, as it propels its 2-3 tonnes along at a swift gallop.

JACKALS

These wild dogs resemble wolves, but they are smaller and have a more pointed muzzle. They can be considered (together with vultures), as the 'dustmen' of the forests and savannas, because they feed on the carrion of animals killed by the large carnivores, on refuse, and on putrefying flesh. They live in large packs, led by a male. They are active at night, and their mournful barking echoes dismally in the darkness. Among the African species are the striped jackal (*Canis adustus*) and the black-backed jackal (*C. mesomelas*).

ALOE

PAPYRUS

DATE PALM
DRAGON TREE

At Aswan, in Egypt, at the first of the six cataracts, the Nile offers an interesting spectacle, even if, after the construction of the famous dams, the cataracts have lost much of their majesty. From afar, the rivers can be seen solemnly advancing between banks of granite and very green countryside. Then, the river slowly becomes filled with hundreds of little islands, covered in luxuriant vegetation.

KALAHARI DESERT

This is the biggest desert in southern Africa and occupies a large part of the territory o Botswana. The Kalahari is more a semi-desert, without surface water but with relatively widespread vegetation that supports nomadic animal life. It lies about 1,000 m above sea level. The sand dunes are the most famous feature of the Kalahari. Of pink, reddish, or brick-red colour (depending on the degree of oxidation), they can be up to 60 m high, held firm by strongly rooted bushes.

KILIMANJARO

In the local tongue, Kilimanjaro means 'the white mountain'; today it has been renamed 'Uhuru' (freedom). It is 5,888 m high and is therefore, truly the roof of Africa. Situated in northern Tanzania, near the border with Kenya, this powerful, volcanic massif dominates the whole of central southern Africa with its two peaks eternally covered in snow. It can be seen 500 km away. The Masa Amboseli Game Reserve, in Kenya, of which i forms the most imposing feature, stretches out at its foot. The principal attraction is the rhinoceros, but all species of large African fauna are to be found in this region, and the bird life is prolific.

KRUGER NATIONAL PARK

This is the most famous and attractive national park on the African continent. It was also the first of its kind in Africa, established in 1898 and expanded in 1926. With an area o 20,000 sq km, it stretches from north to south in north-east Transvaal, along the border with Mozambique, a belt 40-80 km wide and 380 km long. The park is at an altitude varying between 150 and 650 m, and consists of open veld, with low brushwood interspersed with grassy clearings. The climate is entirely continental. What cannot be explained is the mysterious air of suspense that dominates the park. Perhaps it is simply the expectation o finding oneself face to face with elephants lions, leopards and cheetahs, antelopes impalas, zebras, buffaloes, or other grea carnivores and herbivores that inhabit the park.

The genus *Euphorbia,* of the spurge (Euphorbiaceae) family, includes over 1,600 species, distributed throughout the temperate and tropical areas of the globe. Some are native to the continent of Africa. Among the exotic species, many greatly resemble certain cactuses (Cactaceae family). This is a typical case of form convergence, i.e. the adoption of a similar appearance by different plants, such as Cactaceae and Euphorbiaceae, which, when subjected to the same environmental conditions, have adapted in a similar manner to the hot, dry climate. Many species of Euphorbia are cultivated in gardens as ornamental plants.

LAKE KIVU

Lying between lakes Tanganyika and Edward on the Zaïre-Rwanda border, Lake Kivu is the highest lake in Africa (1,472 m) and is one o the many marvels of the Great Rift Valley. No infrequently in this great fissure of the Earth volcanic overflows have blocked the paths o rivers. Here, the Virunga volcanoes have halted the flow of waters in the direction o the Nile, and caused the formation of this very beautiful lake, which has penetrated the narrow valleys of minor rivers to form scenery similar to that of the Norwegian fiords. Even as recently as 1948, a river of molten lava laden with potassium, descended into the lake with a velocity of 36 km/h, causing the water to boil on a huge scale and exterminating all the fish.

NILE

This, the longest river in the world (6,679 km) is also the most famous, because of the grea civilization that flourished on its banks from 3000 BC. The main headstream of the Nile i the Kagera, which flows into Lake Victoria The Victoria Nile flows from the lake, in Uganda, receives the waters from two big lakes (Kyoga and Albert), and takes the name first of the Albert Nile and then of Bahr e Jebel (Mountain Nile), as it crosses through Sudan. From there, the river flows through

Discovered in Angola in 1859, this very strange plant *(Welwitschia mirabilis),* sometimes called the 'miracle plant', has a stem only a few centimetres high, but up to a metre wide. There are just two large leaves, leathery and strap-shaped, and these, as they wear away at the tip, re-form at the base. The leaves, sometimes 3 m long and over 1 m wide, last the whole lifetime of the plant, and that can be a century or more. The plants are either male or female, and bear small, erect spikes of primitive flowers that look like fir cones. The welwitschia grows in the sandy deserts of the coast of south-western Africa. It gets water mainly from sea fogs driven inland by the wind.

marshes and swamps, and would lack water were it not expanded by the contributions of tributaries. The name changes again to Bahr el Abyad, or White Nile, and the river continues losing water until it reaches Khartoum, where it receives the magnificent contribution of the Blue Nile, the great Ethiopian tributary to which it owes its floods.

Nile Delta. About 20 km north of Cairo, the Nile branches off into several channels, flowing into the sea across a front 200 km wide. The area of the delta is 25,000 sq km. The ancient Greeks gave the name 'delta' to the land built up by the Nile, because it is shaped like the capital delta ($\triangle$), the fourth letter of their alphabet. Two of the numerous channels in the delta (Rosetta on the west, Damietta on the east) are navigable to large ships. The other channels irrigate the intensively cultivated and densely populated region.

Nile floods. The waters of the Blue Nile used to produce the famous Nile floods from June to September, floods to which Egypt owes its history and modest well-being. The waters, which come from the mountains of Ethiopia, are laden with mud and humus of volcanic origin, which used to be deposited by the water over a vast area in a layer just a millimetre thick—enough to give the banks of the Nile an exceptional degree of fertility. Nowadays the Nile floods are controlled by the Aswan Dam.

NYIKA

The African name means 'desolate expanse'; naturalists find it a 'hostile and fascinating' land. The area, situated between Kenya and Tanzania, covers hundreds of thousands of square kilometres, and is a dense woodland of brambles and underbrush, thorny acacias and succulent plants, which are both thorny and poisonous. Only during the rains is there a brief flowering, after which everything takes on a bleak and bare appearance, an appearance of death. The temperature is very high and there is no water at all. Only in the Tsavo National Park (20,800 sq km), in Kenya, where the presence of recently formed volcanic rocks gives rise to springs and rivers, is there a rich and varied vegetation. In the fresh waters of the interior live hippopotami and crocodiles. Elephants, rhinoceroses, and lions inhabit the forest.

OSTRICH

The ostrich *(Struthio camelus)* is the biggest of living birds. Once also widely found throughout southern Europe and Asia, the ostrich is now found only in Africa and Arabia. It lives in more or less large flocks, often mixed with zebras, antelopes, and gazelles. Unable to fly, but a very good walker and runner, it moves around continuously in search of food, and voraciously devours whatever happens to come its way—grass, insects, wood, stones (which help grind food for digestion). Ruthlessly hunted in the past for its very valuable wing and tail feathers, the ostrich is now protected by special laws.

PALM TREES (see photograph p.35)

Palms are widespread throughout the tropical and subtropical regions of the world. They are plants of a tree-like appearance, with long leaves forming a bunch at the top of the trunk. As well as the coconut palm *(Cocos nucifera)*, the date palm *(Phoenix dactylifera)* is also well known. This is extensively cultivated in north and west Africa for the sugary fruits which, in many regions, form the basis of human and animal diet. The doum palm, or

Above: Oases. In the desert, where the air is dry, where droughts are prolonged and where the heat is intense, only a scrubby vegetation of tough grasses and low bushes can grow. But where the underground aquifers (water-bearing rock), which are usually very deep, are close to, or actually reach, the surface, the vegetation becomes exuberant. Every oasis is a verdant garden where orange, lemon, and fig trees grow, shaded by palm trees, in their turn offering shade to cereals and vegetable crops. The oases are also important centres for people, where camel-drivers stop to rest and exchange goods.

Below: Among Kenya's many riches, her national parks are something special, for they are among the most beautiful animal reserves in the world. One of the smallest (114 sq km) is Nairobi National Park. It lies just outside the capital, between 1,500 and 1,800 m above sea level. The most beautiful of Kenya's parks, and the richest in tropical wildlife, is the Tsavo National Park (20,800 sq km). It attracted worldwide attention when the protection afforded its elephants allowed them to become so numerous that they began to die of starvation. This created a serious conflict for the guardians of the reserve, who were faced with the problem of game control.

*Left:*Dromedaries. The dromedary, or Arabian camel (*Camelus dromedarius*), together with the Bactrian camel (*Camelus bactrianus*), belong to the Camelidae family. The two species are markedly suited to life in arid and desert regions, both by their characteristic humps, which constitute a reserve of fat, and by sac-shaped extensions in their stomach, which retain water for a long time. The dromedary is not strictly a species of camel, but a particular type of one-humped (Arabian) camel that has been specially trained to run carrying a human rider. Camels have been tamed by man for thousands of years, and no Arabian camels are known to exist in the wild state. But despite this long period of domestication, camels are not willing workers, and they obey commands only grudgingly.

for sailcloth, mats, baskets, etc. From the pith of the stems, thin strips could be obtained which, when dried, interwoven, and compressed, formed a special kind of writing paper. For writing on it, the Egyptians used a sharpened reed dipped in an ink made from lampblack or vermilion. Many very ancient papyri have reached us today in a perfect state of preservation.

ROSE OF JERICHO
In the desert regions of north-east Africa and south-west Asia, a ball of dried-up, inwardly curved twigs can often be seen, carried hither and thither by the wind, during periods of prolonged drought. It is an odd little plant (*Anastatica hierochuntica*) of the mustard (Cruciferae) family, called rose of Jericho or resurrection plant (it owes its name to the Crusades), which, when the rains return, absorbs water and stretches out its branches to germinate rapidly. In its normal state it has stems arranged radially, a few oval, hairy leaves, and small white flowers.

RUWENZORI
On the border between Zaïre and Uganda, between lakes Edward and Albert, rises the powerful natural bastion of Ruwenzori, reaching a height of 5,118 m (Mt Margherita). This eternally snow-capped mountain group is almost always wrapped in mists or clouds. In the language of the local inhabitants, it is called the 'Mountains of the Moon', a name used by the ancient Alexandrian map-maker Ptolemy. The American explorer Henry Stanley used another local name, Ruwenzori (rainmaker). The blanket of forest that covers the sides of Ruwenzori is among the most spectacular in the world, a real equatorial forest. Up to 1,000 m, it consists of a complete tangle of lianas and other plants. Up to 2,000 m, there is savanna, with typical trees such as the acacia and the kaffir-boom, and 3-metre-high elephant grass (*Pennisetum purpureum*) in the valleys. Trees of the wooded stream banks include the flame of the forest (*Spathodea campanulata*) and the wild date palm (*Phoenix reclinata*). Above 3,000 m is montane forest, with red stinkwood (*Pygeum africanum*), the mountain bamboo (*Arundinaria alpina*), and giant lobelias and heathers. An alpine zone (3,500-4,500 m) is dominated by giant lobelias and the moss-covered giant groundsel (*Senecio adnivalis*), and carpeted with silvery-leafed, woody-stemmed

gingerbread tree (*Hyphaene thebaica*), of east Africa and southern Egypt, supplies the so-called 'vegetable ivory', which is made from the very hard, white albumen of its seeds, and is used for making buttons and other objects. The fruit of the doum has the flavour of gingerbread. Palms have a great economic importance, because they supply a whole series of products of considerable value, such as fruit, fats, textile fibres, building materials, and fermented drinks.

PAPYRUS (see photograph p.35)
This is a water plant (*Cyperus papyrus*) of the sedge (Cyperaceae) family. It grows on river banks and swampy ground in tropical Africa, and particularly on the Nile Delta. It has long, narrow, straight stems, bearing great tufts of bracts. In ancient Egypt, papyrus was used

*Below:*The Dallol Salt Plain. Danakil Land, a desert region in the Ethiopian province of Eritrea, is an enormous depression, devoid of vegetation, which displays fantastic natural phenomena. Towards the east, along the Red Sea, it is bordered by a chain of extinct volcanoes. At the foot of the mountains, inland, stretches a deep depression, 116 m below sea level, rich in salt, chalk, and potassium deposits. This is the Dallol Salt Plain, which extends over an area of some 5,000 sq km. In places, towers and pinnacles of basalt rise from the salt.

*Right:*A strange-looking tree of the bombax (Bombacaceae) family, the baobab (*Adansonia digitata*) has a massive, barrel-like trunk, which can reach 10 m or more in diameter. It grows in the dry savanna of tropical east Africa, withstanding even long periods of drought by its ability to store up huge reserves of water in its spongy, swollen trunk. It has oval, slightly acid, sweetish, edible fruit, called 'monkey bread'.

Alchemilla, the mountain lady's mantle. Fauna of the Ruwenzori includes elephants, African buffalo, leopards, chimpanzees, monkeys, and many smaller animals, of which the tree hyrax *(Dendrohyrax arboreus ruwenzorii)* is the most typical.

SAHARA
This is the largest desert on Earth, having an area of about 8 million sq km, more than a quarter of the whole African continent, and extending for over 5,000 km, from the Atlantic to the Red Sea. Contrary to common belief, the sandy part constitutes only the smaller part of it, about 30 per cent. It includes vast rocky areas *(hamada),* areas of sand dunes *(erg),* and pebbly areas *(reg or serir).* The height of the dunes varies, and some are hundreds of metres high. The Sahara is mainly plateau at a height of about 600-750 m above sea level, with three mountain ranges rising to 1,500-3,000 m—the Tibesti (highest peak Emi Koussi, 3,415 m), the Ahaggar, or Hoggar (Tahat, 2,193 m), and the Aïr (1,500-1,800 m). Despite the arid climate and high temperatures (often over 50°C in summer during the day), the Sahara contains very sparse, but highly specialized, flora and fauna. There are many oases, mostly watered by springs fed by underground water.

SEYCHELLES
This is a group of 92 islands and islets in the Indian Ocean, about 1,000 km north-east of Madagascar. The largest island is Mahé (145 sq km). The stable equatorial climate (average 26°-27°C), the marvellous vegetation, which is dominated by various species of palm, and the warm ocean waters have given the island a reputation as the 'ultimate paradise', and have led to its very recent tourist popularity. And although the Seychelles are poor in fauna, many of the mammals, birds, reptiles, fish, and insects found there are so rare as to constitute one of the islands' treasures.

SIMIEN
This is the most spectacular area of the Ethiopian plateau, between the Takazze River and Lake Tana. Seen from the north, from beyond a deep gorge, the plateau appears as an enormous, three-tiered bastion, with towers, escarpments, and domes. These formations create the most remarkable mountain scenery to be seen anywhere in Africa. According to one theory, about 40 million years ago there was great volcanic activity here, of the Hawaiian type, i.e. the lava flowed out slowly, covering vast expanses and taking on dome-shaped forms, up to 1,300 m thick. Later, erosion, caused by torrents and waterfalls, deeply scored the lava, cutting the cliff face into a series of gorges and chasms.

SORGHUM
The sorghums belong to the grass (Graminae) family, and have large grains, tightly clustered on a spike and inclined on the stem. They are extensively cultivated in Africa and India, the grain being ground into a meal for making bread, porridge, cakes, and biscuits. In its raw state it is used as fodder. The chief species of sorghum is *Sorghum vulgare,* with its many varieties; including durra and kaffir corn.

SUDD
One of the biggest swamps in the world, covering an area of several thousand square kilometres, is to be found in southern Sudan, and the White Nile flows through it. It is a

jungle of papyrus reeds and elephant grass. When this vegetable matter collects on the river, it is known as 'sudd', and it becomes so thick that it could hold up an elephant, and sometimes forms a dam 30 km long and 5 m deep. For many years it was the only obstacle hindering exploration of the course of the Nile.

TRAVELLER'S-TREE
This plant *(Ravenala madagascariensis),* indigenous to Madagascar and belonging to the banana family (Musaceae), resembles the palm. Its stem is cylindrical and a large fan of giant oval leaves rises from the top. The common name derives from the tradition that a thirsty traveller could always get a drink of rain water from it by cutting through a leafstalk.

VICTORIA FALLS
These falls are the most famous, and perhaps the most beautiful, in Africa, and one of the largest (by volume) in the world. They are about 120 m high at the centre, the water plunging into a deep, narrow chasm. They are situated on the border between Zambia and Rhodesia, about midway between the source and the mouth of the Zambezi River. The river leaves the chasm through a narrow opening to enter a winding gorge. The falls were named after Queen Victoria by the British explorer David Livingstone in 1855.

VULTURES
These are large birds of prey, belonging to different families, which live on the flesh of dead animals and clean up the environment like 'dustmen'. Among the best-known of African vultures are the Egyptian vulture *(Neophron percnopterus),* very common throughout Mediterranean Africa, and the griffon vulture *(Gyps fulvus),* frequently found in northern Africa and in western and central Asia as far as Turkestan.

The main feature of the savanna is the hot climate, which is constant for the whole year, with droughts that are interrupted only by a brief period of abundant rains that flood the territory. Arid bushes, dry and leathery grasses, some scattered acacias—from the branches of which hang numerous weaverbird nests—and groups of antelope compose a typical picture of the African savanna.

The Kimberley Open Mine, or 'big hole', is about 450 m across and has a circumference of about 1,500 m. A diamond mine, it was closed in 1914. Kimberley, a city roughly in the centre of South Africa, owes its birth and prosperity to the discovery of rich diamond deposits in the area in 1871. Although diamond mining is still important, Kimberley is now known chiefly as a commercial centre.

NORTH AMERICA

The northern four-fifths of North America is occupied by Canada and the United States. Mexico makes up the southern part, and Greenland and Central America are often included in the continent. Viewed from either of the opposite shores of the Atlantic or Pacific, North America (especially the United States) appears to be a continent of huge conurbations, massive industries, and modern motorways, railways, and airports. This image tallies with reality, provided that one is thinking primarily of the shores of the two oceans or of the region of the Great Lakes, or provided that one is simply recalling the overwhelming rapidity of this land's growth. In 1852, men set off from Kansas City, in the centre of the continent, on an audacious journey to the Far West, reaching the Pacific after five months; over a century later, twice the distance, from New York to Los Angeles (5,000 km), can be covered in two days and three nights by train, and in four hours by air.

Has progress therefore overcome natural barriers? Undoubtedly, but it has not eliminated them. The mountains, rivers, lakes, deserts, and canyons have remained more or less intact. Man, having overcome them, has preserved and protected them, and today he seeks them out as the only refuge possible from the soul-destroying effect on humanity of industry and urbanization. Over a territory almost equal in area to the USSR, nature has strewn unparalleled masterpieces: freaks of the Earth, incomparable scenery, natural monuments defying imagination, and areas of wild beauty, protected and, therefore, largely unspoilt by man.

Above: Takakkaw Falls. The northern Rocky Mountains stretch along western Canada. In the states of Alberta and British Columbia they exhibit typically alpine features, arising from the obvious traces of glaciation—U-shaped valleys, morainic lakes, and beautiful waterfalls, such as the Takakkaw Falls, on the Yoho River, British Columbia, which are 380 m high.

A close relative of the European elk, the American moose *(Alces americana)* is found all over Canada and Alaska, and in the United States as far south as Idaho. It is the largest member of the deer (Cervidae) family, standing as high as 2.4 m at the shoulders and weighing as much as 800 kg. Strong and agile, despite its bulk, the moose has enormous horns, shaped like a curved shovel with ragged edges. It lives in marshy woodland and feeds on leaves, shoots, and bark. A strong swimmer, it can face the currents of even torrential rivers. It is very pugnacious, and defends itself with horns and hooves. In the last century, the moose narrowly escaped extinction, but is now protected by law.

Above: Bryce Canyon forms the most spectacular part of Bryce Canyon National Park (146 sq km), in the American state of Utah, about 130 km north of the Grand Canyon of Arizona. Set amidst forests of pine, it is an immense amphitheatre, formed by calcareous rocks on which the elements have acted violently. Rain and desert winds have sculptured towers and pinnacles, likened to giant 'lipsticks', in dozens of shades of red, pink, copper, and almost white.

Grand Teton National Park (1,256 sq km), in north-western Wyoming, is dominated to the west by the Teton Mountains *(left)*. The mountains rise abruptly 1,500 m from the level valley called Jackson Hole. The highest peak, Grand Teton (4,196 m), resembles the Matterhorn, in Switzerland. The Snake River, the chief tributary of the Columbia River, flows through the park.

Right: Sequoia. Widespread in the Tertiary period throughout most of the world, only two species of these evergreen conifers of the Taxodiaceae family remain—the giant sequoia or Wellingtonia *(Sequoia gigantea)* and the redwood *(Sequoia sempervirens),* indigenous to the coastal mountains of California. They are the world's largest trees, and live for a very long time. From a ring count, one redwood has been attributed an age of 3,500 years. The giant sequoia is the bulkiest, the largest specimen having a trunk 11 m in diameter and a height of 89 m. The redwood is the tallest, heights up to 111 m being recorded. Today, sequoias grow, protected, in parks and reserves. Imported into Europe, sequoias are cultivated as ornamental plants.

NORTH AMERICA - PHYSICAL

ASIA

ARCTIC OCEAN

North Pole
3970

Greenland Sea
Jan Mayen
Shetland Is.
Orkney Is.
Faeroe Is.
Iceland
Denmark Strait

Greenland
Mt Forel 3385
King Frederik VIII Land
King Oscars Fjord
Scoresby Sound
Gunbjörn 3700

Aion I.
Wrangel I.
C. Navarin
C. Dezhneva
St. Lawrence I.
Bering Strait (East C.)
Nunivak I.
Pribilof I.
Bristol Bay
Aleutian Is.
Kodiak I.
Gulf of Alaska

Beaufort Sea
C. Barrow
Brooks Ra.
Alaska
Alaska Range
Mt. McKinley 6186
Mt. Logan 6050
Mt. St. Elias 5489
Yukon

Queen Elizabeth Islands
Parry Is.
Banks I.
Victoria I.
Prince of Wales
Boothia Pen.
Baffin Island
Baffin Bay
Davis Strait
Thule

Mackenzie Bay
Mackenzie Mts.
Barren Grounds
Great Bear Lake
Great Slave Lake
Arctic Circle
L. Garry
Chesterfield Inlet
Southampton I.
Foxe Basin

Canadian Shield
Hudson Bay
Hudson Strait
Ungava Pen.
Ungava Bay
Labrador

Churchill
Hudson Bay Lowland
James Bay
La Grande
Laurentian Plateau

ROCKY MOUNTAINS
Coast Range
Columbia Plateau
Cascade Range
Blue Mts.
Great Basin
Sierra Nevada
California
Colorado Plateau
Grand Canyon
Great Salt Lake
Mt. Whitney 4418
Mt. Shasta 4317

Vancouver I.
C. Flattery
Mt. Rainier 4391
San Francisco
Los Angeles
San Diego
Pt. Concepción

Yellowstone National Park
Bighorn Mts.
Black Hills 2176
Front Ranges
Wasatch Ra.
Denver
Mt. Elbert 4401
Blanca Pk. 4386

Great Plains
Interior Lowlands
Missouri
Platte
Kansas
Arkansas
Red
Ozark Plateau
Llano Estacado
El Paso
Pecos
Rio Grande
Colorado

Lake Winnipeg
Winnipeg
L. Manitoba
L. Superior
L. Michigan
Chicago
L. Huron
L. Erie
L. Ontario
Niagara Falls
Ottawa
Quebec
St. Lawrence
Georgian B.

Appalachian Mts.
Allegheny Mts.
New England
Mt. Washington 1914
Boston
New York
Long I.
Washington
Chesapeake Bay
Piedmont
Mt. Mitchell 2038
C. Hatteras
Savannah

Gulf Coastal Plain
New Orleans
Mississippi Delta
Florida
C. Canaveral
C. Sable
Miami

Gulf of Mexico
4376
Corpus Christi Bay
Rio Grande

Newfoundland
St. John's
C. Race
Grand Banks
Gulf of St. Lawrence
Nova Scotia
Sable I.
B. of Fundy
Bermuda Is.

Bahama Islands
Gr. Inagua I.
Havana
Florida Strait
Andros Is.
Cuba
Jamaica
Cayman Is.
Greater Antilles
Hispaniola
Puerto Rico
Central Cordillera 3170
Mona Pass.
Windward Passage
Caribbean Sea

Tropic of Cancer
Guadalupe I.
Sebastian Vizcaino Bay
Cedros I.
Alijos Rock
Revilla Gigedo Is.
C. San Lucas
Tres Marías Is.
C. Corrientes

Lower California
Gulf of California
Western Sierra Madre
Eastern Sierra Madre
Mexican Plateau
Mexico
Popocatepetl 5452
Colima 4340
Citlaltepetl 5700
Tampico

Gulf of Campeche
Yucatán
Gulf of Honduras
Honduras
Tajumulco 4220
G. of Tehuantepec
G. of Fonseca
San Salvador
L. Nicaragua
Isthmus of Tehuantepec
Southern Sa. Madre
G. of Panama
Isthmus of Panama

Clipperton I.
PACIFIC OCEAN
Cocos I.
Malpelo I.

Sierra Nevada de Santa Marta 5775
Maracaibo
Cord. de Merida 5002
Caracas
Curaçao
Pta. Gallinas
Bogotá
ANDES
Western Cord.
Eastern Cord.
Nev. de Cocuy 5493
Llanos
Quito
Chimborazo 6272
Galapagos Is.
Equator
Amazon

ALTITUDES
Metres / Feet
5000 / 16404
4000 / 13123
3000 / 9843
2000 / 6562
1000 / 3281
500 / 1640
200 / 656
Sea level 0
Depression
DEPTHS
0
200 / 656
2000 / 6562
4000 / 13123
More than

Scale 1:34000000
0 250 500 750 1000 1250 1500 Kms.
0 250 500 750 1000 St.mls.

West from 100 Greenwich

Copyright. Vallardi Ind. Graf.

AMERICAN BISON

Widespread in its millions on the prairies of North America until the last century, the American bison (*Bison bison*) is similar in appearance to the European bison, or wisent. In North America, it is miscalled 'buffalo'. The bovids were decimated by ruthless hunting (particularly during the construction of the railway from the Atlantic to the Pacific Ocean), so much so that by the late 1800s the numbers were reduced to a few head. At that time, strict regulations were brought into force for their protection and to prevent their extinction. Parks and reserves were created, in which they have again multiplied, but where they have lost their ancient, proud, and pugnacious character.

BEAVERS

Similar to the Eurasian beaver in appearance and habits, the American beaver (*Castor canadensis*), a rodent of the Castoridae family, is widespread throughout North America along the banks of rivers and lakes. Intelligent and industrious, it is a very able swimmer and constructs its lodge with a long access tunnel, leading from an entrance below the water level. In order to keep the level constant, the beaver skilfully constructs solid dams with tree trunks (real works of engineering). He fells these himself with his very strong incisors, which are as sharp as chisels. Hunted indiscriminately for hundreds of years for its valuable fur, the American beaver is now protected by strict hunting laws.

BIGHORNS

Bighorn is the name by which the Rocky Mountain sheep (*Ovis canadensis*) is commonly known. It is so called because of its large, tightly coiled horns, which are very wide at the base and, in the male, are up to 60 cm long. It is the only living example of the American wild sheep. It lives from Alaska to Mexico in herds of about 50 animals, and has a remarkable ability to climb and jump in the most dangerous places.

CARIBOU

Caribou is the North American name for reindeer. In North America, the caribou (*Rangifer arcticus*) is found, in its many subspecies, throughout the huge area that stretches from the Arctic Ocean to the northern United States. In the summer months, the caribou inhabit the tundra of the extreme north. In winter, they migrate in huge herds towards the woods farther south, walking tirelessly even in snow, prevented by their hooves from sinking in. They always follow the same routes, clearly marked now by their migrations, even in the forests.

CARLSBAD CAVERNS

A huge system of underground limestone caves in south-eastern New Mexico, the Carlsbad Caverns were formed about 60 million years ago, at the same time as the Rocky Mountains. As the area rose above sea level, water began hollowing out the limestone. Huge stalagmites and stalactites in white and cream and pastel greens and blues have formed into fantastic shapes. But perhaps the most remarkable spectacle of all is one that can be seen only at dusk from April to October—millions of bats swarm upwards and out through the natural entrance, in search of insects in the nearby valleys, returning at dawn.

CASCADE RANGE

Along the Pacific coast, the Cascade Range forms a rampart in front of the great chain of the Rocky Mountains. It extends from southern British Columbia in Canada, south through the United States as far as northern California. Streams have cut deep valleys, covered with forests of pine and fir. The mountains consist of volcanic rocks, many of the peaks being extinct volcanoes. Lassen Peak (3,190 m), in California, is the only active volcano on the United States mainland (excluding Alaska). The highest mountains in the Cascade Range are Mt Rainier (4,392 m), in Washington, and Mt Shasta (4,317 m), in California, both of which contain several glaciers.

COTTON (see photograph right)

Probably of Indian (Aztec) origin, cotton is a plant (genus *Gossypium*) of the mallow (Malvaceae) family, and is cultivated in numerous varieties, derived almost exclusively from American species. The textile fibre (lint) consists of the hairs that envelop the seed, and the value of which depends on their length and fineness. As well as the hairs, there is a short fuzz on the seeds called linters, which is used as a source of cellulose and for stuffing, packaging, guncotton, etc. Cottonseed oil is made from the seeds. The cultivation of cotton requires a loose soil, plenty of sun, and frequent rains, with 180 frost-free days in the growing season. When the cotton flower dies, the ovary enlarges, filled with the seeds and their hairs. As the seed ripens, the hairs die and dry into white fibres, which become so bulky that the ovary splits, exposing the cotton boll. The bolls are collected by hand or with appropriate machines. They are then passed into a cotton gin, which separates the cotton from the seeds. The major producers of cotton are the United States, the USSR, China, India, and Brazil.

DOUGLAS FIR

The Douglas fir (*Pseudotsuga menziesii*, formerly *taxifolia*), a member of the pine (Pinaceae) family, is not a true fir, and more closely resembles the spruces. It is the most important timber tree of the forests of North America. Widespread mainly on the Pacific side and in the Rocky Mountains, the Douglas fir is a magnificent tree, reaching heights of 70-90 m, with needle-like leaves, a pyramid-shaped crown, and woody, hanging cones 5-10 cm long. Its wood is easily worked and is used for construction, fencing, panelling, doors, flooring, etc. The straight trunks are used for masts and poles.

GRAND CANYON OF ARIZONA

This is the most magnificent example of erosion in the world. It has been created by the Colorado River, which flows along the bottom of this fantastic valley, 350 km long, 13-32 km wide, and the walls of which reach more than 1,600 m in height. There is little trace of vegetation except on the tree-covered rims, and the rocks lie in horizontal layers in a kaleidoscope of colours, ranging from yellow to red, and changing with the changing light of the sun. Great towers of hard rock stand out from the gorge like ancient temples. It has been calculated that the canyon took 200 million years to form, and the process is continuing.

GREAT LAKES

The mid-eastern region of the North American continent between Canada and the United States is mostly covered by the Great Lakes, linked to the Atlantic by the St Lawrence Seaway and St Lawrence River. The

MAGNOLIA

MAPLE

COTTON
MAIZE

The fifth largest island in the world (476,066 sq km), Baffin Island is part of Canada's Northwest Territories. It is named after the English explorer William Baffin, who anchored there in 1616. Although it is on the same latitude as Greenland, the south is free from ice and snow from July to October and assumes a tundra-like appearance. The features that make the eastern coasts of Baffin Island more closely resemble Greenland and the polar regions are the comparatively low mountains (up to 2,500 m), from which descend imposing glaciers.

height of 60 m, is one of the chief timber trees of the Pacific Northwest, its wood being used for construction work and pulp. The smaller eastern hemlock (*T. canadensis*), which thrives in the vast region stretching from the southern edge of Hudson Bay to the mountains of Georgia, is also used for making paper pulp.

LABRADOR
The land which gives its name to the coldest of all sea currents is the mainland part of Newfoundland, a province of Canada. It seems certain that it was visited in the late AD 900s by the Viking explorer Leif Ericson. The appearance of Labrador is chilling—cold and bleak, with long, severe winters and short, cool summers. Little more than 20,000 people inhabit its nearly 300,000 sq km. The coastline is deeply indented with long fiords, and lined with small islands. Large areas are covered with forests, but the interior is snow-covered from September to June.

MAGNOLIA (see photograph p.43)
Magnolia is a genus of trees and shrubs of the Magnoliaceae family, which can grow up to 45 m. The southern magnolia (*Magnolia grandiflora*) is indigenous to North America, from North Carolina to Texas. An evergreen, it is cultivated the world over in parks and gardens for its majestic bearing, the beauty of its shiny leaves, which are a lovely shade of dark green, and, above all, for its beautiful large white flowers, which bloom all summer and emit a heady fragrance. Magnolia wood, which is soft and yellowish, is used for furniture, the most important timber-producing species being the cucumber tree (*M. acuminata*), which gets its name from the shape of its fruits.

MAPLE (see photograph p.43)
A genus of the Aceraceae family, the maple includes 13 American species, the most important of which is the sugar maple (*Acer saccharum*), very widespread in Canada and in the north of the United States. Much of the sweet sap can be extracted by making holes in the trunk, and this sap is used in the preparation of so-called maple sugar. The tree yields hard, solid wood, light reddish-brown and capable of taking a fine polish. Its uses include furniture, flooring, and fuel.

lakes Superior, Huron, Michigan (wholly in the United States), Erie, and Ontario have a total surface area of 245,000 sq km. The largest, Lake Superior (82,413 sq km), is about the size of Ireland, and is the largest lake in the world (excluding the Caspian Sea). It is the deepest (406 m) and the highest above sea level (180 m). The differences in level between the various lakes have been overcome by means of canals and locks, so that the lakes constitute the biggest internal waterway in the world, vital to the economy of the two countries.

GREAT SALT LAKE
The largest lake of its kind in the Western Hemisphere, Great Salt Lake is in north-western Utah and was once part of a much larger freshwater lake (called Bonneville). Over millions of years it dried up, and is now nearly five times as salty as the oceans. Its area varies with the level of the water, averag-ing nearly 4,000 sq km. Its average depth is about 5 m, and it stands 1,280 m above sea level. There are no fish in the lake, but its islands are breeding grounds for birds such as pelicans, gulls, and cormorants.

GRIZZLY BEAR
Resembling the European brown bear, but heavier and more stocky, the grizzly bear (*Ursus horribilis*) has a characteristic brown coat streaked with grey or silver. It lives in the forests of northern America, from Alaska to California, protected in national parks and reserves.

HEMLOCK
The hemlocks are graceful conifers of the pine (Pinaceae) family, resembling the fir, and are widespread in two different and well-separated areas, eastern Asia and the coastal regions of North America. The western hemlock (*Tsuga heterophylla*), which grows to a

There are over 3,000 hot springs in Yellowstone National Park, Wyoming. Mammoth Hot Springs *(left)* have built up a series of terraces covering 8 sq km and are as much as 100 m high. The water, which is crystal clear, deposits limestone over the surface, and the beautiful colours are due largely to algae.

Right: The petrified forest in northern Arizona is not the only one in the world, but it is perhaps the most attractive. Prehistoric trees, buried in the mud, have been subjected to a slow, natural process by which silica, molecule by molecule, has replaced wood and cellulose, transforming them into solid stone.

MISSISSIPPI DELTA

This is one of the most interesting regions of the North American continent, because of its rapid and continual transformation. It 'grows' into the Gulf of Mexico at the rate of 1 km every 10 years, because the river's slow current is continually depositing mud, sand, and gravel there. The area of the Mississippi Delta is about 90,000 sq km, much of it rich, fertile and. In ancient times, the river flowed in a south-westerly direction before it entered the sea, but because of the continuous subsidence of the ground and the subsequent invasion by the sea, the river gradually shifted eastwards until it formed the present peninsula, with its characteristic bird's-foot shape. The whole region is a marvellous tangle of lakes, rivers, channels, and tree-covered marshes.

MISSISSIPPI RIVER

Between the great mountain ranges that border the United States along the Atlantic and Pacific coasts stretch the Interior Plains, watered by the Mississippi or its tributaries. The source of the river is at an altitude of only 450 m, yet it flows for a distance of 3,780 km, which demonstrates the slowness and majesty of this great watercourse. With its tributaries, it drains about a third of the area of the United States. Its chief tributary, the Missouri, is the longest river in the country (4,380 km), and together they form the third longest (after the Nile and Amazon) river system in the world (6,230 km).

MONTEREY CYPRESS

The Monterey cypress (*Cupressus macrocarpa*) is native to California, has a flat and expanded crown, and is cultivated in Europe as an ornamental garden tree. One of the most picturesque trees in North America, it grows on storm-swept shores, gnarled and bent by strong ocean winds, its massive branches growing into unusual shapes.

MONUMENT VALLEY

Of all the changing and remarkable scenery of the Colorado basin, this valley in south-eastern Utah and north-eastern Arizona is one of the most outstanding. The ancient plateau of reddish sand has been eroded over thousands of years by the winds, causing rocky formations up to 300 m high to emerge. In the evening, one of these monumental buttes of sandstone casts a shadow 56 km long.

MOUNT McKINLEY

The highest peak in North America, Mt McKinley (6,194 m) lies in central Alaska, in the Alaska Range. Some 300 peaks of this range dominate the southern edge of the Mt McKinley National Park, a region rich in animal life, including moose, caribou, Dall sheep, and over 130 species of birds.

NIAGARA FALLS

The most famous falls in the world, on the border between Canada and the United States, the Niagara Falls are on the Niagara River, which links the waters of lakes Erie and Ontario, between which there is a difference in level of 99 m. Although neither the biggest nor the highest in the world, they are certainly among the most spectacular. The Horseshoe Falls, on the Canadian side, are 640 m wide and 57 m high; the American Falls are 335 m wide, 59 m high. The edge of the Horseshoe Falls is being worn away by the pounding of the water by about a metre a year, and of the American Falls by about 10-20 cm.

Above: A typical feature of Arches National Monument. This extraordinary area of desert and shrub in eastern Utah was established as a national monument (138 sq km) in 1929. It contains spectacular rock formations caused by wind erosion that has contrived to bore through huge blocks, sculpturing them into domes and pinnacles and forming arches, the work of hundreds of millions of years.

Right: The White Sands National Monument (593 sq km) is situated in southern New Mexico. It consists largely of huge deposits of gypsum sand, blown by the wind into 'dunes' 3-15 m high. In bright sunlight, the blinding-white sands look like a vast snowfield.

About 10 species of poplars, which include aspens and cottonwoods and belong to the willow (Salicaceae) family, are native to North America. They thrive in moist places and grow rapidly. Their wood is light and soft, and is used to make boxes and crates and in the plywood and paper pulp industries. Quaking aspens *(Populus tremuloides, right),* which are common in Canada and the United States, fill in rapidly on mountain slopes that have been burned over. Their leaves extend from long, flattened stems and 'tremble' in the slightest breeze.

Big Bend National Park (2,866 sq km), a wilderness of desert and mountains, lies in the 'big bend' of the Rio Grande in Texas, on the border with Mexico. The Chisos Mountains were created by ancient volcanic eruptions and shaped by erosion. They reach a height of 2,388 m and are surrounded by vast stretches of desert. The park's wildlife includes bighorn sheep and the Sonoran deer.

Below: The two most important species of tobacco, which belongs to the nightshade (Solanaceae) family, are *Nicotiana tabacum* and *N. rustica.* Cultivated by the American Indians prior to Columbus's voyage of discovery, tobacco was introduced into Portugal and Spain in the mid-1500s and from there spread to the rest of Europe and to the other continents. The name *Nicotiana* is in honour of Jean Nicot, the French ambassador to Portugal, who is said to have sent the tobacco plant as a gift to Catherine de Médicis, the queen of France. Tobacco is cultivated in countries with warm temperate climates. The major producers are the United States, followed by China and India.

OKEFENOKEE SWAMP

This primitive swamp in America stretches over an area of about 1,800 sq km on the border between the American states of Georgia and Florida. It is covered with thick deposits of peat, and includes marshy savannas, low, sandy ridges, several marsh-bound islands called 'hummocks', and lakes covered with small bushes and floating weeds. The swamp was once a hunting ground of the Seminole and Creek Indians, and the name is a corruption of an Indian word meaning 'the place where the earth trembles'. Any disturbance of the topsoil is enough to set the vegetation 'trembling'. About three-quarters of the swamp (in Georgia) has been set aside as a wildlife refuge, and its fauna includes alligators, racoons, bears, deer, and otters, and over 200 species of birds, including ibises and wild turkeys.

OLD FAITHFUL

Yellowstone National Park (9,000 sq km), America's oldest and largest, is situated in the north-western corner of Wyoming and overlaps into Idaho and Montana. Of the many natural wonders it contains, perhaps the most famous is the geyser called 'Old Faithful'. It is not the largest of the 200 geysers in the park, but has become famous for its regularity. In displays lasting about 4 minutes, its silvery cascades of nearly boiling water shoot up 35-50 m in the air, on an average every 65 minutes (varying from 33 to 93 minutes), night and day, every day for more than 100 years since it was first discovered.

PAINTED DESERT

The Colorado basin, the most dramatic part of the Rocky Mountains, is a real kaleidoscope of striking natural scenery. The so-called 'Painted Desert' is a vast area of low

Right: The bald cypress *(Taxodium distichum),* a conifer of the Taxodiaceae family, is so called because, unlike most conifers, it sheds its leaves in winter. It is a majestic tree, which grows along water-courses in the marshy areas of the south and east of the United States, from Texas to New Jersey. It grows to a height of 30-40 m, and has a pyramidal crown. It is characterized by its 'knees', which it thrusts up out of the water and which supply air to the submerged roots. The trees in the picture are in Cypress Gardens, the beautiful natural park on Lake Eloise, Florida.

hills, the tops of which have been rounded off by the erosive action of wind and water. The region stretches for some 300 km, and the brilliant reds and yellows are due to the presence of iron oxides, red from haematite and yellow from limonite. The heat, light, and dust also affect the colours, which include pastel blues, lilacs, and greens, in an ever-changing pattern that seems to have been painted by a giant brush.

PEACE PARK

In full, the Waterton-Glacier International Peace Park, this is situated on the border between the United States and Canada, in the states of Montana and Alberta. It was established in 1932 by combining the Waterton Lakes National Park (500 sq km, in Alberta) with the Glacier National Park (4,100 sq km, in Montana). It lies in the Rocky Mountains, and the Continental Divide runs through the centre from north to south. It is a beautiful, unspoilt area.

POPOCATEPETL

Popocatepetl—'smoking mountain' in the ancient language of the Aztec—is one of the great volcanoes of the Mexican plateau and one of the largest on earth. It is an almost perfect cone, and the well-shaped crater yawns open at a height of 5,452 m above sea level. Its top is permanently covered with snow, and the lower slopes are green with conifers. At its foot grow palm, orange, and banana trees. Clouds of smoke and gas pour from its mouth, but the last major eruption occurred in 1702. Its neighbouring twin, Ixtacihuatl (5,286 m), provides a striking contrast, its Aztec name meaning 'the sleeping lady'.

PRAIRIE DOGS

These are rodents of the *Cynomys* genus of the squirrel (Sciuridae) family. They live in innumerable colonies on the prairies of the Midwest of the United States, and are found in most parts of western North America. They dig underground tunnels, dozens of kilometres long, in which they take refuge from danger and store up food for the winter months. They are a serious pest to farmers, and are hunted and poisoned. They eat grasses and roots, and their burrows can cause horses and cattle to stumble.

ROCKY MOUNTAIN GOAT

Similar in size to the domestic goat, the Rocky Mountain goat *(Oreamnos ameri-*

canus) has a characteristic pure-white coat of bristly hair and soft fluff. It belongs to the cattle (Bovidae) family, but is not a true goat (genus *Capra*), and is more closely related to the antelopes. Although numerous last century, on mountains in the west of North America, by the beginning of the 20th century it was reduced to a few individuals, owing to ruthless hunting, primarily for its warm coat. It now lives on mountains between 2,000 and 4,000 m in remote and impenetrable regions. It has also been put in reserves to encourage breeding.

ROCKY MOUNTAINS
The Rocky Mountains stretch for about 5,000 km along the western part of North America, from Alaska to New Mexico, and form one of the largest natural bastions on earth. The jagged, snow-covered peaks have been shaped by the elements over millions of years, and glaciers have hollowed out the valleys. The lower slopes are grassy, with great forests of pine and spruce giving way to shrubs higher up. The highest point of the Rockies is Mt Elbert (4,399 m), in the Sawatch Range, in Colorado.

SANGRE DE CRISTO MOUNTAINS
These are part of the Colorado Rocky Mountains, a terrible region of barren and scorched mountains, of isolated and extinct volcanoes, interconnected by great blackish walls formed by the lava outflows of millions and millions of years ago. The name is Spanish for 'blood of Christ', and they are so called because at sunrise the snow-capped peaks take on a reddish appearance. The range extends for about 340 km through southern Colorado and northern New Mexico. The highest point is Blanca Peak (4,364 m). West of the mountains, in the San Luis Valley, a curious phenomenon is to be found—light-brown sand dunes, up to 450 m high. These have been deposited over thousands of years, swept along by the wind and piled up against the mountains. The Great Sand Dunes National Monument covers an area of 149 sq km.

SIERRA NEVADA
Between the Rocky Mountains and the Pacific, in the United States, stretches the Great Basin. In the west it is enclosed by impenetrable walls, a screen of rock between the coast and the interior, consisting of two mountain chains, the Cascade Range and the Sierra Nevada. The Sierra Nevada is the more impenetrable and majestic of the two. It stretches for some 650 km along eastern California and is 60-110 km wide. Its highest peak, Mt Whitney (4,418 m), is the highest in the United States outside Alaska.

VALLEY OF TEN THOUSAND SMOKES
Alaska, land of gold and oil, is also a land of active and extinct volcanoes of great geological interest. The Aleutian Range forms the backbone of the Alaskan Peninsula, which extends from southern Alaska westwards to the Aleutians, a chain of volcanic islands that stretch for 1,500 km into the Pacific. The greatest eruptions in the Aleutian Range occurred in 1912, when a new volcano, Novarupta, hurled masses of ashes and rocks into the air. The top of another volcano (Mt Katmai) collapsed, forming a basin over 1,000 m deep. The surrounding area within a radius of over 20 km was covered with ash and lava, and millions of jets of steam (fumaroles) issued from the valley floor, giving the Valley of Ten Thousand Smokes its name.

Above: Death Valley. This is a depression, as much as 86 m below sea level (the lowest point in the Western Hemisphere). It lies in east-central California, near the border with Nevada, and is a trough about 210 km long and 10-20 km wide. It is lined on either side by mountains, with canyons formed by erosion. Temperatures in summer regularly exceed 50°C. In glacial times, the valley was filled by a large lake.

Below: Probably originating in Mexico, maize *(Zea mays),* also called Indian corn, is now extensively cultivated in the United States and in many other parts of the world. It is a cereal of the grass (Gramineae) family and requires hot summers and plenty of rain. The kernels are used for many types of food. The main kinds of maize have different kernels and include sweet corn, popcorn, dent corn, and flint corn.

SOUTH AMERICA

Above: The Cordillera Real is a range of the central Andes in Bolivia, extending north-west to south-east, just east of Lake Titicaca and La Paz, the capital. The range displays great flanks of bare, hard rocks, which have been deeply scored by torrents. In the background rise the snow-capped peaks of Nevado Illimani, the powerful massif, 6,882 m high, that towers over La Paz.

Left: The Iguaçu River, a left-bank tributary of the Paraná, flows along the border between Argentina and Brazil. About 23 km from its confluence with the Paraná, the Iguaçu widens to about 4 km and drops over about 20 cataracts separated by rocks and tree-covered islands, forming the Iguaçu Falls, the most spectacular waterfalls on the continent of South America. The average drop is over 60 m, and in the rainy season the waters are tinted by the region's red soil. The waterfalls are on the border of three countries—Argentina, Brazil, and Paraguay—all of which have created national parks in the area.

Right: The cacao, or chocolate, tree *(Theobroma cacao)* grows wild in the Amazon and Orinoco basins, but even before Columbus 'discovered' America, it was cultivated in Mexico by the Aztecs. The rich Mexicans were very fond of a drink obtained from the seeds of the plant. At one time, the seeds, or cacao beans, were used as money. The cultivation of cacao, possible only in tropical regions, spread from Central to South America, and then to other continents. The tree grows to a height of about 8 m, and the fleshy fruits, which may be 30 cm long, hang directly from the trunk. The beans are used to make cocoa and chocolate products.

It is difficult to discuss South America without thinking of it as part of Latin America, which also includes Central America and Mexico. If we really wish to understand this part of the world, we cannot ignore the importance of Latin civilization, Spanish and Portuguese, past and present, for a civilization also ends up by constructing a particular landscape, shaping the land and directing the economy. In the 1800s, when the greatest power on earth was already taking shape, in North America, the countries of Latin America were acquiring their own independence, at the cost of a sometimes drastic splintering of their natural unity. Only the English, Dutch, and French presence resisted this tendency, and still does so in the Antilles.

Despite political events, the continent is still unified by its geography as well as its history. The symmetry of the southern and northern continents is remarkable. At both ends of the very long isthmus linking the coastal mountains of the North and South Pacific, there are two clearly differentiated regions: to the west, facing the Pacific, is a large chain of mountains, a barren landscape with active volcanoes. This is in sharp contrast to the huge plains in the east, furrowed by the enormous rivers that flow into the Atlantic.

In Central and South America, the mountains are second in the world in height only to those of Asia. The plains are green deserts—green from the trees of the Amazon forest or the grass of the pampas and Patagonia. The rivers are on a similarly large scale. It is enough to quote a few figures: the Andes chain stretches along almost half a hemisphere, a distance of 7,250 km, from Panama to Tierra del Fuego; the pampas constitutes the greatest plain on earth, with an area of some 750,000 sq km; the tropical rain forest of the Amazon covers an area 3,000 by 2,500 km; and the River Amazon is nearly 6,300 km long, is fed by over 200 tributaries, and drains an area of about 6.5 million sq km.

Llamas, which belong to the camel (Camelidae) family, are indigenous to South America, and are, well adapted to high altitudes. The guanaco *(Lama guanicoe)* and the vicuña *(Lama vicugna)* still exist in the wild, the latter possessing very valuable wool, which was formerly reserved for the emperor and his family during the time of the Incas. The lama proper *(Lama glama)* is a domesticated form of the guanaco. It has been a beast of burden for thousands of years, and provides wool and meat. It was the basis of the Inca economy, and they sent messages over thousands of kilometres by tying a complicated series of knots (quipu) in the long, shaggy fur hanging from the underside of the animal. The alpaca *(Lama pacos)*, another domesticated form, also provides wool, and lives in the mountains of Peru and Bolivia, especially round Lake Titicaca.

The dense forests of South America provide the best habitat for myriad birds of the most varied sizes and habits, particularly remarkable for their strange shapes and gaudy plumage. The most beautiful and brightly coloured parrots *(right)*, which make up the Psittacidae family, live in South America *(Ara* and *Amazona* genera). Both the hummingbird, a minute, gaudily coloured bird that makes up the Trochilidae family, and the toucan, which belongs to the Ramphastidae family and is characterized by its enormous brightly coloured beak, also live in the South American forests.

SOUTH AMERICA - PHYSICAL

Gulf of Mexico
Florida
C.Sable
Miami
Gt. Abaco
Florida Strait
Andros Is.
Long I.
Havana
Cat I.
Acklins I.
Bahamas
Gt. Inagua
Cuba
I. of Pines
Cayman Is.
Jamaica
Hispaniola
Puerto Rico
Virgin Is.
Greater Antilles
Leeward Is.
Guadeloupe
Martinique
Dominica
Barbados
Windward Is.
Grenada
Margarita
Trinidad
Lesser Antilles

Yucatán
C.Catoche
Yucatán Str.
Gulf of Honduras
C.Gracias a Dios
Segovia
Honduras
Vol. Tajumulco 4220
S. Salvador
G. of Fonseca
L. Managua
L. Nicaragua
Volcán Irazú 3433
Azuero Pen.
G. of Panama
Isthmus of Panama
Panama
C.Mariato
Cocos I.

Caribbean Sea

ATLANTIC OCEAN

Tropic of Cancer

Pta. Gallinas
Guajira Pen.
Paraguaná Pen.
Curaçao
Bonaire
G. of Venezuela
Sa. Nevada de Santa Marta 5775
L. Maracaibo
Cord. de Mérida
Caracas 2765
Coast Ranges
Georgetown
Cayenne

PACIFIC OCEAN

Malpelo I.
C.San Francisco
Galapagos Is.
Isabela
Sta. Cruz
Equator

Western Cord.
Central Cord.
Eastern Cord.
Cord. de Mérida
Magdalena
Bogotá 5215
Tolima
Huila 5750
Volcán Cayambe 5790
Quito 4896
Cotopaxi 6272
Chimborazo
Guayaquil
G. of Guayaquil
Pta. Pariñas
Pta. Aguja
Lobos Is.
Huascarán 6768
Lima

Llanos
Orinoco Basin
Apure
Orinoco
Meta
Guaviare
Vichada
Guiana Highlands
Roraima 2772
Sierra Pacaraima
Sa. Parima
Sa. Tumucumaque
Serra Imeri 2450
Sa. Pacaraima

Caquetá
Putumayo
Napo
Marañón
Yavari
Ucayali
Javari
Juruá
Purús
Madre de Dios
Beni
Mamoré
Guaporé
Amazon Basin
Selvas
Amazon
Negro
Branco
Japurá
Manaus
Marajó I.
Belém
São Luis
Equator
St. Peter and St. Paul Rocks

Montaña
Eastern Cordillera
Serra dos Parecis
Tapajós
Xingu
Tocantins
Araguaia
Sa. da Desordem
Rocas I.
Fernando de Noronha
C.São Roque
C.Branco
Recife
Borborema Plateau

Titicaca 6615
Illampu 6362
Illimani 6462
La Paz
Sajama 6520
L. Poopó
Bolivian Plateau
Coropuni
Yungas
Plateau of Mato Grosso
Bananal I.
Sa. Geral de Goiás
Brasília
Brazilian Highlands
Campos
Sertão
Caatinga
São Francisco
Jequitinhonha
Pico da Bandeira 2890

Tocopuri 6755
Desaguadero
Atacama Desert
Antofagasta 8066
V. Llullaillaco 6723
P. San Francisco 4722
Ojos d. Salado 6380
Tucumán
Gran Chaco
Pilcomayo
Bermejo
Asunción
Paraguay
Iguaçu Falls
Itatiaia 2821
São Paulo
Rio de Janeiro
C.Frio
Trinidad
Martin Vaz Is.

Tropic of Capricorn
Desventurados Is.
S.Felix
S.Ambrosio
Juan Fernandez Is.
Salinas Grandes
Sa. de Córdoba
Córdoba 2880
L. Mar Chiquita
Rosario
Paraná
Salado
Entre Rios
Uruguay
R. Negro
Sa. de Maracaju
Campos
Porto Alegre
Sa. do Mar
Lagoa dos Patos

Aconcagua 6960
Valparaíso
Vol. Maipo 5323
Salado
Pampas
Buenos Aires
Montevideo
River Plate (Río de la Plata)
L. Mirim

Coast Ranges
Colorado
Bahía Blanca
Blanca Bay
Valdivia
Tronador 3554
L. Nahuel Huapi
R. Negro
G. of San Matías
Valdés Pen.
Rawson
Chubut

Chiloé I.
Chonos Arch.
Taitao Pen.
S. Valentin 4058
Wellington I.
Queen Adelaide Archipelago
Patagonian Cordillera
Patagonia
L. Buenos Aires
G. of St. George
C.Tres Puntas
Grande Bay
Falkland Is. (Islas Malvinas)
Strait of Magellan
Punta Arenas
Tierra del Fuego
Sta. Inés I.
I. de los Estados (Staten I.)
C.Horn
Drake Passage
South Georgia
Shag Rocks
South Sandwich Is.

ALTITUDES
Metres / Feet
5000 / 16404
4000 / 13123
3000 / 9843
2000 / 6562
1000 / 3281
500 / 1640
200 / 656
Sea level
Depression

DEPTHS
0
200 / 656
2000 / 6562
4000 / 13123
More than

Scale 1:34000000
0 250 500 750 1000 1250 1500 Kms.
0 250 500 750 1000 St. mls.

Copyright: Vallardi Ind. Graf.

AGAVE (see photograph right)
About 300 species belong to this genus of the daffodil (Amaryllidaceae) family, distributed throughout Mexico and the adjacent areas as far as California, the Antilles, the Bahamas, and Venezuela. A very tough fibre (sisal) can be obtained from the leaves of *Agave sisalana* and other species cultivated on large Mexican plantations. This fibre is used for making coarse cloth, mats, sacks, and ropes.

AMAZON RIVER
The second-longest river in the world (to the Nile), the Amazon flows for nearly 6,300 km, from north-eastern Peru, through Brazil, to the Atlantic, draining an area of some 6½ million sq km. By volume, it is far and away the biggest river in the world, disgorging as much water in one day as the Thames does in one year, and its current can be seen 200-300 km out in the Atlantic.

ANDES
A direct continuation of the North American system, the Andes form the most extensive mountain bulwark in the world, stretching for some 7,250 km along the entire west coast of South America, from Panama in the north to Tierra del Fuego. It is an enormous rampart, against which the tempests of the Pacific Ocean exhaust their strength. Its origin lies in the great phenomenon of the uplifting and folding of the ocean floor, which took place between the Secondary and Tertiary periods. The principal feature of the Andes, the result of the violent nature of their birth, is the presence of many, still active, volcanoes. The highest peak is the extinct volcano Aconcagua, 6,960 m above sea level, in Argentina, near the border with Chile. It is the highest point in the Western Hemisphere.

ANGEL FALLS
The south-east of Venezuela consists of high plateaus called La Gran Sabana, covered with thick forest and deeply scored by rivers. Rushing over the edge of a high plateau, about 2,500 m above sea level, a tributary of the Caroní River forms Angel Falls (Salto del Angel), the highest known waterfall in the world. It is 979 m high, including an unbroken drop of 807 m, and is 150 m wide at the base. The falls are named after an American flyer and adventurer, Jimmy Angel, who crash-landed his plane nearby in 1937.

ANTEATERS
These are among the strangest mammals in South America, and make up the family Myrmecophagidae. In the areas where ants and termites are dangerously numerous, anteaters play the important role in the food-chain of preventing certain groups of insects from breeding to excess. The giant, or great, anteater (*Myrmecophaga tridactyla*) is native to the tropical grasslands of South and Central America, and can reach a length of 2 m, about a third of which is tail. Its long, cylindrical muzzle allows it to penetrate anthills and termitaries, after breaking into them with its big strong claws. Its long, worm-like and sticky tongue completes the task, gathering insects, eggs, and larvae. The lesser anteater, or tamandua (*Tamandua tetradactyla*), about half the size of the giant anteater, is more widespread and much more common. It spends most of its time in trees, feeding on termites and ants that build their nests there. The nocturnal, rarely seen pygmy, or two-toed, anteater (*Cyclopes didactylus*) is about the size of a squirrel and lives in the trees of the tropical forests.

ANTILLES
Columbus called here on his first journey in 1492, and on his second journey he explored these islands, which were marked on the oldest maps as the West Indies, but they do not include the Bahamas. They consist of a continuous chain of islands, stretching in a wide arc round the Caribbean Sea for over 3,000 km, from the Yucatán Peninsula (Mexico) to the coast of Venezuela. They are divided into two groups—the Greater Antilles and the Lesser Antilles. They are all volcanic. The volcanoes of the Greater Antilles are extinct, those of the Lesser Antilles active. Exploration of the sea bed has revealed that the Antilles are the emerging peaks of large, submerged mountains. While enjoying a climate of eternal springtime, the islands are subject to hurricanes of unparalleled violence.

ARAUCARIA
This genus of conifers includes evergreen trees with scaly or acicular leaves, and is widespread throughout South America, Australia, and Oceania. The Paraná pine (*Araucaria angustifolia*) forms large forests in central and southern Brazil. The monkey puzzle tree (*A. araucana*) prospers on the Andes in southern Chile as far as the snow-line, and is cultivated elsewhere as an ornamental tree.

ATITLAN
In Guatemala, the volcanic chain of mountains offers the visitor not only the spectacle of the perennial fire of its volcanoes, but also the enchantment of intensely blue lakes, reflecting the incandescent peaks. The most attractive of the lakes is Lake Atitlán, 39 km long, 16 km wide, and occupying a crater 300 m deep, surrounded by three volcanoes. It lies at an altitude of 1,430 m, and has no known outlet. In the ancient Maya language, the name means 'abundant waters' and, according to legend, the waters renew themselves perennially, changing colour as they do so.

BARRO COLORADO
The central section of the Panama Canal crosses the huge Gatun Lake, which contains several islands. The biggest island, Barro Colorado (15 sq km), which became an island when the waters rose as a result of the cutting of the canal, is only 135 m above water and is completely covered by tropical forest. It is a forest that is a microcosm of Central America—trees up to 40 m tall, more than 250 species of birds, big cats (puma, jaguar, ocelot), and other mammals (monkeys and tapirs). Today, the whole island is an area for scientific study and research, sponsored by a Washington institute of science.

CASSAVA
These plants of the *Manihot* genus of the spurge (Euphorbiaceae) family are native to tropical South and Central America and have been cultivated since before the age of Columbus for their tuberous roots, which supply edible flour. At present they are cultivated in tropical west Africa, Malaysia, and Indonesia, and are an important food crop in tropical regions. In the sweet varieties, the tubers can be eaten raw, like potatoes. In the bitter varieties, containing a toxic substance (prussic acid), the tubers must be reduced to a paste and washed thoroughly. After cooking in fresh water, the starch forms small lumps known as tapioca, which is used in puddings, etc. Cassava is also called manioc.

ORCHID

AGAVE—SISAL

PINEAPPLE

COFFEE—FLOWERS AND FRUIT

Much of Colombia, named after Christopher Columbus, is covered in tropical forest, an excellent habitat for all tropical flower species, including splendid orchids. Apart from its natural wonders, the forest of San Agustín is famous for its ancient civilizations. This fascinating archaeological area, first discovered in 1914, nestles nearly 1,400 m above sea level between ridges of the Colombian Andes. Tombs, stone temples, and anthropomorphic statues have been found scattered throughout the forest, some of them dating back to the 500s BC.

24°C all year. Numerous varieties are produced from *Coffea arabica*, the principal species. The major producer of coffee is Brazil.

GALAPAGOS ISLANDS

Discovered in 1535 by the Bishop of Panama Tomás de Berlenga, the Galapagos Islands consist of about a dozen main islands and numerous islets, lying along the equator about 1,000 km off the coast of Ecuador, to which they belong. Though they have little economic or strategic importance, they are of great interest, for their formation and especially for their unique wildlife. They are all volcanic islands, consisting of volcanic cones emerging from the sea either singly or in linked groups. The main island is called Isabela (4,270 sq km, over half the total land area), and is formed by five volcanoes. The islands look like beautiful prisms of dark or luminescent lava, with sides falling away sheer into the sea, offering very little scope for anchorage. Water, too, is very scarce, and vegetation is therefore minimal, except on the upper slopes of the volcanoes (up to 1,500 m), which are surrounded in mists. The Galapagos Islands were among the areas studied by Darwin during his famous voyage on the *Beagle* in 1835, and helped to inspire his theory on the evolution of the species. He was impressed with the curious features of the animals and plants, all having certain characteristics that distinguished them from their mainland relatives. The Galapagos are an ideal place for the study of evolution isolated as they are in the ocean, and the harshness of the land making it necessary for the few chance colonists to adapt very quickly to their new environment. Some of the more interesting fauna include the birds, the turtles, and the iguanas. The birds include a flightless cormorant, a penguin, and several species of finches that behave like other birds, such as the woodpecker finch, which uses a twig or cactus spine to probe for food. The giant turtles, which weigh as much as 250 kg, gave the islands their name, *galápago* being an old Spanish word for turtle. But perhaps the most dramatic are the iguanas especially the docile marine iguana (*Amblyrhynchus cristatus*), which can grow to a length of 1.5 m and is the only known lizard that habitually frequents sea water.

IRAZÚ

Costa Rica, in Central America, is a land of towering volcanoes, hot coastal plains, and high tablelands. In the central mountain range stands Irazú (3,432 m), an active volcano. It has a unique feature in that, from its summit, on a clear day, it is the only place on the North and Central American continent where it is possible to see both the Atlantic and Pacific oceans.

LIGHTHOUSE OF THE PACIFIC

Just in from the coast of El Salvador, in Central America, lies a low range of mountains, volcanic in origin, dominated by a number of higher peaks. One of these is Izalco (1,185 m), created in 1770 by a violent eruption. Since then it has been intermittently active, and is called 'the Lighthouse of the Pacific' by sailors, who can see its flames and smoke far out at sea.

MAHOGANY

Mahogany is a valuable red wood. Strong and hard, yet easy to work, it polishes to an attractive high lustre and is used in the manufacture of luxury furniture. Trees of the

CINCHONA

Among the exotic plants used in pharmacy, those of the various species of the *Cinchona* genus, of the Rubiaceae family, have held an important place since the 1600s. Various drugs can be extracted from the bark of these trees, which are indigenous to the Andes from Bolivia to Colombia, including quinine, which is used for treating malaria.

COFFEE (see photograph p.51)

This is the name given to both the plant (Rubiaceae family) and the fragrant beverage that is obtained from the dried and roasted seeds. Originating in Ethiopia, the coffee plant spread to Arabia and Turkey and, from there, in the 1660s, to Italy and the rest of Europe. The Europeans spread its cultivation to Asia, Africa, and the Americas, in mountainous tropical areas with high humidity and in which the temperature might average 18-

Above left: The Andes are a source of immeasurable wealth (still not exploited) and of natural beauty (not yet completely discovered). Some of the highest peaks of the Andes are in Bolivia, and enclose some of the biggest lakes on the continent and present natural features of great beauty. One of these is on the east side of the mountains, near La Paz—the Valley of the Moon. The name comes from the contorted shapes of the rocks, eroded by wind and water, so that they take on a lunar appearance.

Kapok is the name for the whitish, light, soft fibres that cover the seeds of a few plants of the bombax (Bombacaceae) family. The best-known of these is the silk-cotton tree *(Ceiba pentandra)*, a large (up to 30 m), fast-growing tree, indigenous to South America. Kapok fibres are short and weak, and are therefore not suitable for spinning and weaving, but they are perfect as stuffing material.

Meliaceae family, the most important true mahoganies are the scarce West Indian mahogany (*Swietenia mahagoni*), which produces the finest wood, and the Honduras mahogany (*S. macrophylla*), which comes from the rain forests of northern South America.

MARACAIBO
Lake Maracaibo is Venezuela's treasure chest. Situated at the centre of a huge depression, stretching along the Caribbean coast, it was covered by the sea in ancient times. It extends to the Gulf of Venezuela through a long, narrow neck. The lake (16,300 sq km) is the largest in South America, but would be a desolate and insignificant sheet of water had oil not been discovered there, hidden beneath the alluvial deposits of very early times. Today, oil is the basis of Venezuela's economy, and the country is one of the largest producers in the world.

MONKEYS OF THE AMAZON
The monkeys that live in the Amazon forest are characterized by their small or medium height, their long, slender limbs, their thick fur, and often by a prehensile tail. They are all tree-living, and may be subdivided into two families: the Cebidae, which include the capuchins, squirrel monkeys, spider monkeys, and howling monkeys, and the Hapalidae, which include the marmosets and tamarins.

NAHUEL HUAPÍ
This national park (7,900 sq km in area), which takes its name from one of its beautiful lakes, Nahuel Huapí, stretches across the northern region of Patagonia, in Argentina, near the border with Chile. The contrast in vegetation is marked, ranging from pampas in the east to alpine scenery and flora on the slopes of the Andes. Fauna include the pudu deer, Andean condor, and cormorant. The park is dominated by the peaks of the volcanic El Tronador (3,472 m), the name of which (The Thunderer) stems from the great roar of thawing blocks of ice as they plunge down to Lake Frías.

ORCHIDS (see photograph p.51)
In the hot, damp forests of the tropical areas of America grow thousands of species of orchids (Orchidaceae family), either on the ground or as epiphytes on the bark of trees. They have gaudy, strangely shaped blooms with fascinating shades, and they often emit a heady perfume. Orchids have developed a very specialized dependence on insects for pollination, many of them being limited to a single species of insect or even to just one sex of a species. Among the most famous orchids of South America are those of the many varieties of the *Cattleya* and *Epidendrum* genera.

ORINOCO
One of the great rivers of South America, the Orinoco is over 2,000 km long. It rises in south-east Venezuela, near the border with Brazil, and after a few hundred kilometres it suddenly displays an unusual phenomenon —the Casaquiare branches off on the left, a natural channel that flows in the opposite direction to the Orinoco, linking it, via the Rio Negro, with the Amazon. The Orinoco itself continues to flow north-west, and then north, as it forms part of the border with Colombia, then east, right across central Venezuela to the Atlantic; the whole course makes an enormous C-shaped sweep. The river and its

numerous tributaries drain four-fifths of Venezuela and a quarter of Colombia, and its great delta is frequently flooded in the rainy season.

PAMPAS
This is the biggest plain on earth, stretching across central Argentina, from the Atlantic coast to the foothills of the Andes, merging into Patagonia in the south and the Gran Chaco to the north, with an area of about 750,000 sq km. It may be divided into two distinct areas—the dry pampas on the west, poorly irrigated and largely barren, and the humid pampas on the east, where the rivers re-emerge from underground to form lagoons. Most of the region is flat, formed of soil that has been eroded from the Andes and has accumulated over millions of years. The resultant fertile, grassy, treeless plain forms the most extensive pastures for cows and sheep in the world.

Above: The Mato Grosso is the huge plateau which, from the depths of the interior of Brazil, slopes gently down towards the Amazon forest. With an area of $1\frac{1}{4}$ million sq km at a height of 600-900 m above sea level, the Mato Grosso is a tangle of vegetation (its name means 'large forest') and quicksands, the undisputed kingdom of wild beasts and deadly insects. In the southern, more fertile region, the agricultural exploitation of the land has begun with plantations of coffee and sugar-cane and impressive cattle ranches.

Right: Sugar-cane (*Saccharum officinarum*) is a plant of the grass family that has been cultivated since olden times in India and China. The Arabs introduced it into the Mediterranean basin, and it was taken to America from Spain in the 1500s. At present, it is cultivated in all the hot, damp regions of the world, including Brazil, the West Indies (especially Cuba), and Colombia. From the stems (2-5 m high), which are shredded and crushed, is obtained a syrupy liquid from which are extracted crystallized sugar and molasses.

Two-fifths of the area of Brazil is covered by the largest forest in the world, the Amazon forest. It takes its name from the Amazon River, which crosses it from west to east and, with its tributaries, waters the whole area. The vast, undulating, evergreen expanse has at all times a hot and damp climate. The huge trees grow at a prolific rate, linked to each other by an impenetrable tangle of lianas. The trees are the kingdom of magnificent birds, insects, and monkeys and other wild animals. In the waters lives the common spectacled caiman *(Caiman sclerops)*, a voracious crocodilian that rarely exceeds 2 m in length. In this 'desert' of vegetation, man is almost absent (one inhabitant every 2 sq km). Towns and villages are to be found only along the rivers, which are all navigable. Today, attempts are being made to cut roads, although these are difficult to maintain because of the speed with which the forest spreads.

PUMA
Also called the cougar or mountain lion, the puma *(Felis concolor)*, which belongs to the cat (Felidae) family, resembles a lioness in appearance. It adapts easily to a great variety of places and climates, living both in the open prairies of the plains and in the dense mountain forests, in well-watered areas and in extremely arid regions. A skilful and agile climber, the puma surprises birds and monkeys among the tree branches, attacking also deer and sheep from above.

RIO NEGRO
The major left-bank (northern) tributary of the Amazon, the Rio Negro flows for about 2,250 km, mostly through Brazil, after rising in eastern Colombia. The main feature of the river, and the reason for its name (Black River), is the dark colour of its waters, caused by the organic substances that they contain. The rivers of the Amazon basin have distinct colours, ranging from the Negro (which is more red than black), through bluish-green, to yellowish-white. The meeting of the Amazon and the Negro is a remarkable sight. As the dark water of the Negro runs into the light water of the Amazon, the two flow side by side with a clearly visible line of demarcation between them for some 80 km, before the greater volume of the Amazon, with its 'white' water, prevails.

ROSEWOODS
This is the name of tropical evergreens of the *Dalbergia* genus (Leguminosae family), which produce a very hard, attractive ornamental wood, ranging in colour from dark reddish- to purplish-brown. The name comes from its roselike fragrance when freshly cut. Brazilian rosewood, or blackwood *(D. nigra)*, is used for cabinet-making, Honduras rosewood *(D. stevensonii)* for such items as xylophone bars and knife handles.

SIERRA NEVADA DE MERIDA
In the north of the continent, this is an extension of the Andes, also called the Cordillera Mérida. It crosses north-western Venezuela from south-west to north-east, from the Cordillera Oriental to Caracas and the coast. The highest point is Pico Bolivar (5,000 m). The slopes of the mountains are farmed for cereals and coffee.

Below: The Atacama Desert stretches along northern Chile to the border with Peru. One of the driest deserts in the world, it is a huge, sandy expanse in which, however, nature has placed large copper deposits. It stretches, between the mountains in the east and the plateaus in the west, for about 1,000 km. It has a meteorological observatory that has never yet recorded any rain.

PATAGONIA
One of the world's most extensive sheep-grazing areas, Patagonia is a dry plateau of Argentina and Chile. Much of it is desert, and large deposits of oil and iron ore have been found. The name comes from a Spanish word meaning 'big feet', referring to the native Indians who wore huge boots stuffed with grass.

PINEAPPLE (see photograph p.51)
A plant of the pineapple (Bromeliaceae) family, the pineapple is the fruit of the *Ananas sativus* species, cultivated in Mexico, Florida, the Antilles, Malaysia, and, particularly, in Hawaii. The fruit has a fleshy, juicy, slightly acidic and fragrant pulp. Originally native from Paraguay to Mexico, the plant was reintroduced into the Americas and elsewhere as a seedless variety with larger fruits, developed in English greenhouses.

Right: The cactus (Cactaceae) family is one of the most distinctive in the plant kingdom, and includes most of the succulent plants that are widespread throughout the desert areas of the Americas, Africa, and the Mediterranean region. The plants of the cactus family are xerophytes (that is, suited to arid soils); they exhibit characteristic forms of adaptation for storing large amounts of water and for preventing evaporation; and they have fleshy green stems, and leaves transformed into spines. Among the best-known is the giant saguaro *(Cereus giganteus)*, in the photograph.

SNAKES

A great quantity of snakes of different species, sizes, and habits live in South America, a continent rich in dense forests, swampy regions, and habitats suitable to reptile life. The anaconda *(Eunectes murinus)* is a snake of the boa (Boidae) family, the largest living snake, over 8 m long. It lives on the river banks and in pools in the equatorial and tropical forests, and it kills its victims underwater and swallows them. Also common in South America are the poisonous pit vipers, which make up the Crotalidae family. They include the cascaval or tropical rattle-snake *(Crotalus durissus)*, the fer-de-lance *(Bothrops atrox)*, and the bushmaster *(Lachesis mutus)*.

TIERRA DEL FUEGO

The southern region of South America is broken up into numerous peninsulas, among which the sea traces gulfs and fiords. The Strait of Magellan can also be considered as a very long fiord, the natural link between the Atlantic and Pacific oceans. South of the strait is Tierra del Fuego, a group of islands that owe their name to the fires lit by the Indians to warm themselves and to disperse the mists descending on the region. The main island, also called Tierra del Fuego, has an area of 50,000 sq km, and is divided into two distinct sections. The Andes extend through the western part, which belongs to Chile, and the plateau of Patagonia extends through the eastern part, which belongs to Argentina. The coastal plains are bleak, and the climate is cold in winter and cool in summer. Most of the northern part of the main island is under 200 m high, whereas the rest of the archipelago is mountainous, with peaks of over 2,000 m and glaciers. In Argentine territory, in the south of the main island, on the Beagle Channel, is the southernmost town in the world, Ushuaia.

TITICACA

Lake Titicaca lies among the tallest peaks of the Andes, straddling the frontier between Peru and Bolivia. At an altitude of 3,812 m, it is the highest large body of water in the world, and it has an area of 8,446 sq km. The lake is notorious for its icy waters and the dreadful storms that rage across it. Civilizations grew up round the lake even before Inca times, and today the shores are crowded with Indian villages. The people retained their customs despite Inca and Spanish conquests.

VANILLA PLANTS

These are climbing plants (*Vanilla* genus) of the orchid family, indigenous to tropical America, and extensively cultivated in Mexico, Madagascar, and Réunion. A fragrant essence (vanillin) is obtained from the fruit, which is gathered while still unripe and submitted to artificial fermentation. This essence is used in the flavouring of liqueurs, chocolate, cakes and sweets, ice creams, and also in perfumery and certain tobacco products.

VICTORIA REGIA

A species of giant waterlily (Nymphaeaceae family) growing in the Amazon basin, *Victoria regia* was imported into England and named in honour of Queen Victoria. It has giant, round, floating leaves with an upturned rim that gives it the look of a circular pan. In its native habitat, the leaves can reach 2 m in diameter and support a small child. The starry pale-pink flowers blossom at night, opening just above the water. They may grow as much as 45 cm wide.

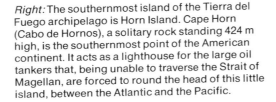

The central section of the Andes Mountains spans the equator, and contains a chain of volcanoes, many of which are still active. Cotopaxi *(above),* in Ecuador, is 5,896 m above sea level and the highest active volcano in the world. Nearly a perfect cone, it is covered with glaciers and snowfields.

Right: The southernmost island of the Tierra del Fuego archipelago is Horn Island. Cape Horn (Cabo de Hornos), a solitary rock standing 424 m high, is the southernmost point of the American continent. It acts as a lighthouse for the large oil tankers that, being unable to traverse the Strait of Magellan, are forced to round the head of this little island, between the Atlantic and the Pacific.

Penguins make up the Sphenisciformes, an order of birds that have such unusual physical features as to make them unlike any other bird. They have a squat body, wings incapable of flight (they have developed into flippers which serve as paddles), and webbed feet on which they walk erect. Penguins live in the Antarctic regions and southern waters, spending a great part of their life in the sea. They go onto dry land only in order to breed, forming multitudinous colonies. They care tenderly for their young, the parents taking turns to feed them, until they are able to fend for themselves.

OCEANIA

The vast area of the Pacific that is often called Oceania includes the continent of Australia and all the other far-flung islands that belong to the three broad groups of Melanesia, Micronesia, and Polynesia.

Since its discovery some 200 years ago, Australia has been known as the 'newest continent'—that is, the latest one to be known to civilized man. The expression is historically correct, but geographically and geologically inaccurate. Indeed, Australia is the oldest continent in the world. Once it became detached from the other lands, something like 200 million years ago, the local flora and fauna continued to evolve independently, isolated from external influences and affected only by the natural evolution of species and general world upheavals, such as the ice ages. That is why the continent, with its mountains and deserts, has an 'ancient' appearance. That is why animals that we classify as 'living fossils' are so common there, as also are species that are not found elsewhere. Even the Australian aborigine displays the same degree of civilization as his Stone Age ancestors.

The complete opposite is true for the islands that make up the rest of Oceania. These are extremely young, and many are still being formed. The great number of volcanic or coral islands that make up Melanesia, Polynesia, Micronesia, and the Hawaiian Archipelago are no more than the visible phenomena of a giant folding in the unfathomable depths of the Pacific Ocean. On the surface, corals gather slowly to form the characteristic atolls. And the exploding volcanoes present dramatic firework displays.

Above: Mount Olga is the most composite of the giant monoliths that are scattered over the central Australian desert, north of the Musgrave Range. It consists of a pile of about thirty enormous rocks, the tallest of which soars upwards for 458 m. All these rocks are rounded and have smooth sides, like enormous eggs. Sunset transforms their colour to bright red.

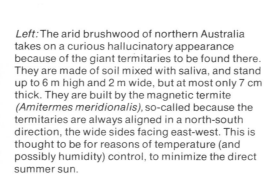

Left: The arid brushwood of northern Australia takes on a curious hallucinatory appearance because of the giant termitaries to be found there. They are made of soil mixed with saliva, and stand up to 6 m high and 2 m wide, but at most only 7 cm thick. They are built by the magnetic termite *(Amitermes meridionalis),* so-called because the termitaries are always aligned in a north-south direction, the wide sides facing east-west. This is thought to be for reasons of temperature (and possibly humidity) control, to minimize the direct summer sun.

Above: Coral islands are limestone formations built up by the 'skeletons' of millions of tiny sea animals (polyps). They have many forms, including mound-shaped 'domes' or the typical ring-shaped atolls. The Great Barrier Reef is a chain of coral islands that extends for 2,000 km off the east coast of Australia, and is 70 km wide in places.

Left: The Australian Alps, in the south-east of the continent, are the southern part of the Great Dividing Range, or Eastern Highlands. They contain Australia's highest mountains, including the 2,230-m Mt Kosciusko, and are a popular area for winter sports.

Right: Tree ferns (Cyateaceae family), typical of virgin, equatorial forest, have a majestic appearance with their tall stems crowned by a halo of leaves, as gigantic as palm leaves. They grow in the humid forests of Australia and New Zealand. The species *Dicksonia antarctica* is common in New Zealand, with a trunk as much as 6 m tall and fronds 2 m long.

57

EPIPHYTES

EUCALYPTUS

WATER LILIES
AUSTRALIAN GRASS-TREE (BLACKBOY)

ATOLLS

The Pacific Ocean is littered with thousands upon thousands of islands, grouped into vast archipelagos that make up the three island areas of Oceania—Micronesia, Melanesia, and Polynesia. There are two main types of islands: the volcanic islands, such as Tahiti and Hawaii, and the low-lying coral islands. The latter generally form a ring-shaped island, called an atoll. This circle, completely enclosed or else cut by a narrow channel, surrounds a lagoon of brackish water at its centre.

AYERS ROCK

From the midst of the central desert of Australia, an extensive plain of reddish earth in the Northern Territory, rises the isolated block of red sandstone called Ayers Rock. It is the largest monolith in the world, an enormous humped rock, of irregular shape, 335 m high, 2.4 km long, and with a girth at its base of about 8 km. Not even a blade of grass grows upon it, although there is relatively lush vegetation round its base. After rain, Ayers Rock offers a magnificent spectacle, as superb waterfalls form and disappear with magical speed. Even the colour of the rock changes quickly, according to the different light conditions and reflections, from deep purple to brilliant orange. It is undercut with eroded caves, which contain aboriginal rock paintings in charcoal and ochres.

BLACKBOY (see photograph left)

The blackboy is the popular name for the Australian grass-tree *(Xanthorrhoea* genus) of the lily (Lileaceae) family. A curious-looking, slow-growing tree (a 3-m tree may be 1,000 years old), it has a trunk topped with a mass of tuft-like foliage and a tall flower stalk as much as 4 m high, with a dense cylindrical spike of small flowers. The name comes from its resemblance (especially when the trunk has been charred by a bush fire) to a grass-skirted figure brandishing a spear.

BLUE LAKE

The city of Mount Gambier, in the south-eastern corner of South Australia, lies on the steeply rising slopes of a former volcanic cone. Lakes have formed in the craters, and one of them, Blue Lake, provides the city with its water. About 80 m deep and only 0.7 sq km in area, it is a brilliant blue in the height of summer, but for some unexplained reason the waters turn a slate-grey the rest of the year.

BLUE MOUNTAINS

The most beautiful area in the Great Dividing Range, the mountains that stretch along the Australian continent to the east, lies behind Sydney. The Blue Mountains are a broken sandstone plateau covering about 1,400 sq km and rising to 1,100 m in the west. The name comes from the pure blue hue of the haze, believed to be due to the effect on the light of tiny droplets of oil from the eucalyptus forests that cover most of the slopes. The flanks of the cliffs are sheer and beautifully coloured—white, red, and yellow. The gorges are deep, narrow, and covered in very dense vegetation, making an even greater contrast with the rocks. Wind and water have produced spectacular forms of erosion, such as the sharp peaks of the 'Three Sisters'.

BORA-BORA

Many Pacific islands are atolls—that is, dense coral reefs surrounding a lagoon. The island of Bora-Bora, in the Leeward Islands, a group in the Society Islands, French Polynesia, has an ancient volcano, 700 m high, situated within the atoll lagoon. The island is inhabited by about 1,500 people, who make their living by fishing and growing vanilla and coconuts; they returned to Bora-Bora after World War II, during which the Americans used the island as a base. The forest is now devouring the war buildings, and the island is reverting to its appearance of a miniature heaven on earth.

BOTTLE TREE

Bottle tree is the common name for various trees native to Australia, genus *Brachychiton,* the trunks of which have a characteristic bottle shape. Most notable is the bottle tree of Queensland *(B. rupestris),* which grows to a height of 15 m and may have a girth of 10 m. The trunk is greatly swollen by sap, which was used by aborigines to quench their thirst.

EPIPHYTES (see photograph left)

Epiphytes are plants that live on others, not parasitically, but for support. They grow in the rain forests, and include some ferns and orchids.

FIORDLAND NATIONAL PARK

Situated in the south-west of South Island, Fiordland is the largest and wildest of New Zealand's national parks, covering an area of 12,234 sq km. It includes mountain forests, lakes, rivers, and waterfalls as well as fiords. Sutherland Falls, the fifth highest in the world, has a drop of 580 m in three leaps. The water eventually flows into Milford Sound (25 km away), a majestic fiord with high, stark walls glistening with snaking waterfalls. The park is the only habitat of the takahe *(Notornis mantelli),* a large flightless bird believed to be extinct until it was rediscovered in 1948, and of the kakapo *(Strigops habroptilus),* an owl-like nocturnal parrot.

FLINDERS RANGE

This barrier of low mountains north of the city of Adelaide is a great South Australian tourist attraction. The peaks of red and purple rocks are the glory of these mountains. At the southern end of the chain, the peaks are covered with a mantle of pines, eucalyptus, and grass, while the steep gorges are edged with white eucalyptus. The most exciting spot is Wilpena Pound, an isolated quartz plateau in the north of the range, a basin surrounded by jagged, vividly coloured peaks and sheer walls. The north wall, St Mary's Peak (1,189 m), is the highest point of the range.

GREAT BARRIER REEF

To the east of the Australian continent, from New Guinea to the Tropic of Capricorn, the Great Barrier Reef stretches for some 2,000 km. Situated 15-250 km off the coast, it is formed by an almost continuous bank of coral, a marvellous submarine wall rising from the continental shelf. The ocean crashes against the barrier with colossal waves, producing a spectacle that can be seen nowhere else in the world.

KIWI

There are only three species of kiwi, a shy, flightless bird found in New Zealand. They make up the Apterygidae family. The best known is the common brown kiwi *(Apteryx australis),* about the size of a chicken. Nocturnal birds, kiwis live in the forests and feed on worms, insects, berries, and leaves. They are the only birds with nostrils at the tip of their bill.

The Wolf Creek Crater, the largest meteorite crater in Australia, is located in the Great Sandy Desert, 96 km south-west of Hall's Creek, Western Australia. Discovered in 1947, it has a diameter of 850 m, with a level floor on which trees grow. One of the least known and most barren parts of Australia, the Great Sandy Desert lies on a vast artesian basin (the Canning Basin).

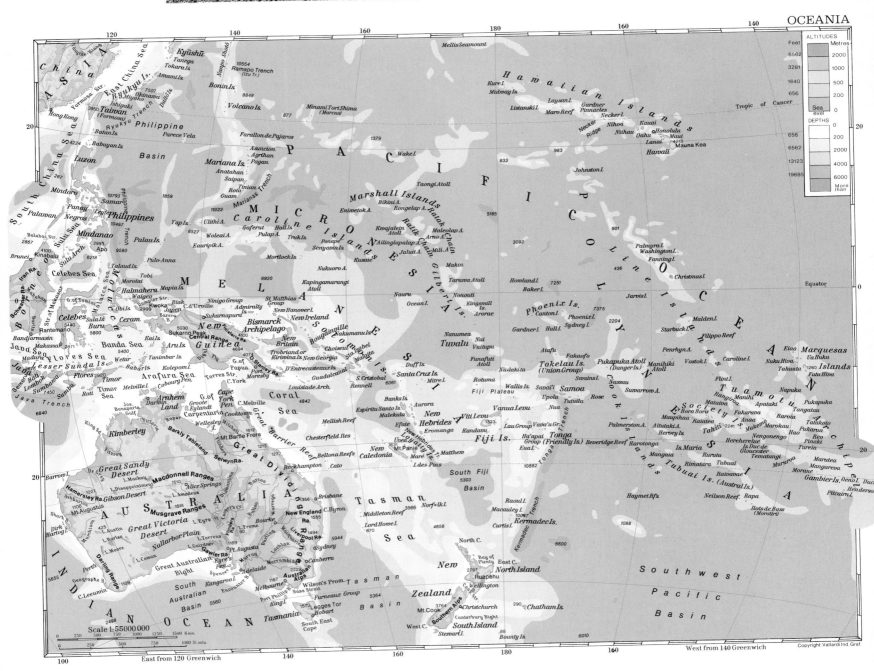

Above: A genus of the myrtle (Myrtaceae) family, eucalypts, or gum trees (so-called because of the resin that exudes from their trunk) as they are commonly known, are evergreen trees or shrubs largely indigenous to Australia and Tasmania, with a few species in New Guinea. They cover 90-95% of Australia's forests, and there are more than 500 species, ranging from the 90-m mountain ash *(Eucalyptus regnans)* to the dwarf mallee species. *Eucalyptus* means 'well covered', and refers to the cap or calyx, the tight cover which remains over the stamens until they open. The distinctive leaves of the eucalyptus are usually bluish-green, long, and pointed, and give off a heady aroma. They contain an aromatic oil, which is used medicinally in the treatment of colds and catarrh.

Below: Kilauea is an active volcano on the island of Hawaii, the largest of the Hawaiian islands. It lies on the eastern slope of Mauna Loa, a larger volcano, in the Hawaii Volcanoes National Park, created in 1916. Its crater, over 3 km in diameter, is 120 m deep, and its rim stands 1,243 m above sea level. During its 1959 eruption (shown in photograph), molten lava was hurled to a height of 300 m.

KOALA

An attractive marsupial of the Phalangeridae family, indigenous to eastern Australia, the koala *(Phascolarctos cinereus)* resembles a small bear and has a large head with big hairy ears, a stocky body, and thick fur. This gentle and timid creature lives off certain species of eucalyptus, feeding exclusively on their leaves and shoots, so that the koala itself smells strongly of eucalyptus. Once slain in large numbers for their fur, they are now protected by law.

KOOKABURRA

The largest representative of the kingfisher family (Alcedinidae), the kookaburra or laughing jackass *(Dacelo gigas)* gets its name from its loud braying 'laugh'. It is native to Australia and New Guinea, and lives on frogs, lizards, small snakes, young birds, fish, insects, and worms. Kookaburras are up to 40 cm long, and live in tree holes.

LAKE EYRE

Vast dried-up salt lakes are a characteristic feature of the southern region of Australia. Rivers flowing from the Great Dividing Range find difficulty in reaching the lakes, and are dried up by the desert sands. Water returns to the lakes only when the rains are particularly heavy. The largest lake is Lake Eyre, at the centre of a depression, 12 m below sea level. It covers an area of about 9,000 sq km, in two basins, the northern being about seven times as large as the southern one. Since records have been kept, it has only once been filled with water, in 1950, and it dried out in two years.

LAMINGTON NATIONAL PARK

This Australian park covers a 200-sq-km area of the Macpherson Range, 110 km south of Brisbane. It is a marvellous mountain region, ranging from 600 to 1,200 m, with escarpments to the south and gentle slopes to the north. The tropical forest is very luxuriant, encouraged by the plentiful rains and sub-tropical climate. While the underbrush is subject to the harsh law of natural selection (the sun hardly penetrates), there are vigorous climbing plants, and orchids hang in clusters from the branches of trees. At the higher levels, the branches of antarctic beech support clumps of staghorn and elkhorn ferns as well as orchids. A great variety of birds inhabit the park, including the rare albert lyrebird and the rufous scrub bird.

MARSUPIALS

Marsupials are mammals whose young are raised in a pouch. This pouch is a pocket, situated on the lower abdomen, in which the young, born in an almost embryonic state, complete their development. Marsupials were the dominant mammals in the Mesozoic Era all over the world. Now most marsupials live only in Australia, Tasmania, and New Guinea. The Australian marsupials include kangaroos, wombats, Tasmanian wolves, koalas, and bandicoots.

MAUNA LOA

Hawaii, the largest (10,458 sq km) of the Hawaiian islands, was formed by five volcanoes. Mauna Loa, or 'long mountain' (4,170 m), although not quite the highest of them, is the largest mountain in the world in cubic content, and discharges more lava than any other volcano. The crater at the top is called Mokuaweoweo, and has a circumference of 8 km. Most of the lava flows from the sides of the mountain.

MONOTREMES

The strangest and most primitive mammals on earth, monotremes are real 'living fossils', displaying features belonging to reptiles and birds, as well as those proper to their own class. Unlike other mammals, they lay eggs. They have a cloaca (a single cavity into which both the intestinal and urogenital tracts open) and a horny beak instead of teeth. Indigenous and exclusive to Australia, Tasmania, New Guinea, and certain neighbouring islands, they include the duckbill or platypus *(Ornithorhyncus anatinus)* and the echidna or spiny anteater *(Tachyglossus aculeatus)*.

RABBITS

Wild rabbits *(Oryctolagus cuniculus)* belong to the Leporidae family and are smaller than hares (rarely exceeding 45 cm in length or 1.5 kg in weight). They multiply prolifically, and their propensity for ravaging grazing land, fields of crops, and the bark of trees makes them a serious pest. Originally, rabbits did not exist in Australia. In 1859, a few common rabbits were imported and returned to the wild, and multiplied at such a rate that they became a serious problem, threatening the whole economy of the continent. Teams of hunters were formed, and these were paid a bounty for each animal killed. Even bacteriological warfare was used, consisting of the spreading of the virus disease myxomatosis, in the early 1950s. This was reasonably effective at first, but the emergence of rabbits resistant to the disease, and the suffering caused by it, suggested the need for a more effective, less cruel, method.

ROTORUA

A spa town in the North Island of New Zealand, Rotorua is the hub of the hot springs area, which extends down to Lake Taupo. The whole area is a mass of trembling earth and boiling lakes, where the mud bubbles and the geysers hiss and roar with steam. The main attraction is the Pohutu geyser, at Whakarewarewa ('the place of rising steam'), which plays irregularly several times a day to a height of 20-30 m for 30-40 minutes.

SEA-LIONS

These carnivores of the eared seal family (Otariidae) are known as sea-lions because the adult males of some species display a thick mane down their neck and shoulders, reminiscent of that of a lion. They are mammals, perfectly suited to the aquatic life, and live in large groups, prevalent in the Southern Hemisphere. The *Zalophus lobata* species is common in the Bass Strait between Australia and Tasmania.

SOUTHERN ALPS

South Island, the larger of New Zealand's two main islands, is traversed in the west, for almost its whole length, by the imposing chain of the Southern Alps. Formed up to 500 million years ago, they were shaken by gigantic earth movements, as evidenced by their knife-edged or pointed peaks. As many as 200 peaks are perpetually covered in snow. The major ones are Mt Cook, 3,764 m high (see photograph right) and Mt Tasman, 3,498 m. The glaciers are huge, among them being the Tasman Glacier, 29 km in length and 2 km wide. Magnificent forest vegetation covers the western face, beaten by the winds.

TUATARA

A 'living fossil', the tuatara *(Sphenodon punctatus)* is the only surviving member of the reptile order Rhyncocephalia, common during the Mesozoic Era. The other members, such as the dinosaurs and iguanodons, became extinct about 100 million years ago. This little lizard, which measures up to 60 cm in length, survives only on a few islands in the Cook Strait, off the coast of New Zealand's North Island, and is rigorously protected by the government.

WATER LILIES (see photograph p.58)

Elegant water lilies grow wild in stagnant waters. Only the flowers and leaves appear on the surface.

WATTLES

Most of the 600 species of the *Acacia* genus (Mimosaceae family) are native to Australia, where they are called wattles. In some of the Australian species the leaflets are dropped and the green petioles expand to take on the shape and function of leaves. Most acacias are evergreens, and many are shrubs rather than trees. The golden wattle *(Acacia pycnantha)* is the national tree and flower of Australia. Also widely grown are the green wattle *(A. decurrens)* and the black wattle *(A.d. mollissima)*.

The coast of the state of Victoria, in the south-eastern corner of Australia, is for the most part high and rocky and is eroded by the very strong winds that blow across Bass Strait, between the mainland and the island of Tasmania. Sometimes erosion produces real masterpieces of sculpture, such as the magnificent limestone rocks called the Twelve Apostles *(above)*.

Right: Wallaby is the name for various marsupials of the kangaroo (Marcropodidae) family, which live on the plains of Australia, Tasmania, and New Guinea. They look like the kangaroo proper, but are smaller, from ½ to 1 m in height. They have a small head, short front limbs, long and sturdy hind legs, and a short coat. Wallabies are fast runners and strong jumpers, able to leap several metres.

Mount Cook, the highest mountain (3,764 m) in New Zealand, lies in the Southern Alps of South Island. Called Aorangi by the Maoris, it is comparable to the most beautiful Alpine summits in Europe, as it stands majestically covered in ice and eternal snows, with a retinue of other silent and immaculate peaks.

INDEX

INDEX OF ENTRIES AND PICTURES
(Italic numbers refer to pictures)